St. Benedict
(from the painting by Sassoferrato at Perugia)

THE RULE OF
St. Benedict

St. Benedict

Translated with an Introduction
by
CARDINAL GASQUET

DOVER PUBLICATIONS, INC.
Mineola, New York

Bibliographical Note

This Dover edition, first published in 2007, is an unabridged republication of the work published by Chatto & Windus, London, in 1925. The present translation is based on an English translation published in 1638. The original work is thought to have been composed about 528 A.D.

Library of Congress Cataloging-in-Publication Data

Benedict, Saint, Abbot of Monte Cassino.
    [Regula. English]
    The rule of St. Benedict / St. Benedict ; translated with an introduction by Cardinal Gasquet. — Dover ed.
        p. cm.
    Originally published: London : Chatto & Windus, 1925.
    ISBN 0-486-45796-6
    1. Benedictines—Rules. I. Title.
BX3004.E6 2007
255'.106—dc22

2007000744

Manufactured in the United States of America
Dover Publications, Inc., 31 East 2nd Street, Mineola, N.Y. 11501

Introduction

The *Rule* of St. Benedict may fitly find a place in any collection of classics. As a code of laws it has undoubtedly influenced Europe; and, indeed, there is probably no other book, save of course the Holy Bible, which with such certainty can be claimed as a chief factor in the work of European civilization. It is undeniable that most of the nations of modern Europe were converted to the Christian faith and tutored in the arts of peace by the influence of the mode of life known as monastic. The men whose names are connected with the beginnings of civilization in the various countries of Europe, and their fellow-labourers, were for the most part trained for their mission under the Rule of St. Benedict. Such, for example, was Augustine in England, Boniface in Germany, Ansgar in Scandinavia, Swithbert and Willibrord in the Netherlands, etc.

In view of the facts, therefore, it will hardly be denied that the monastic system, as codified in the Rule of St. Benedict, has been proved to possess some strange power of influencing great bodies of men and winning them from the darkness of paganism and the horrors of savagery to the light of Christianity and the blessings of a civilized life. The secret of this fascination is obvious, and the monuments, such as Canterbury and Fulda, Salzburg, and the thousands of Benedictine abbeys which existed, or still exist, in Europe, all testify to the fact that it was the monastic life lived by monk-apostles in the midst of the peoples they hoped to convert, upon which their success mainly depended. The monastic plan was similar to the old Roman plan of civilizing by means of "colonies" planted among the conquered races of the empire. The colonists brought with them the arts, and to some extent the culture, of Imperial Rome, and their mere life lived among the subjugated peoples induced these latter of their own accord to adopt the manners, the language and the law of their conquerors. There was probably no programme, or pretence, but the influence of the life followed by the trained Roman colonist worked its charm without noise or compulsion.

In the same way the monk came with the like lesson of peace and civilization, but with the addition of the all-powerful assistance of religion and the strong attraction which self-sacrifice ever exerts over the minds of the unlettered. Thus Augustine came to England which forty companions, all trained in the "school" of St. Benedict, and in the principles of his Rule. They landed in this country and won it to Christ with cross and banner and religious chants. Then they settled down to live their lives of prayer and labour, and whilst their success is written in the annals of our country, we know the names only of a very few of these apostles, and they those only who were called later to form similar centres in other parts. History can tell us nothing of their preaching and teaching. No doubt they did all this; but what we know of their work is that they lived their life according to the Rule; they built up other places and formed other colonies, and then they died; and, behold! the peoples among whom they dwelt were Christian.

ST. BENEDICT

St. Benedict, the author of this code of monastic rules, to the influence of which Europe owes so much, was born at Nursia, a city of Umbria, in the year 480. The beginnings of his life witnessed the extinction of the Roman Empire in the West, and the year of his birth saw Odoacer, the first barbarian who had ruled in Italy, in possession of the throne of the Cæsars. All over the Western world the times were difficult and the outlook gloomy, and Italy especially presented a sad spectacle of misery and desolation. At a time when civilization appeared to be upon the very verge of extinction, and the Christian Church seemed to be on the point of losing the foothold it had gained amid the ruins of the Roman Empire, St. Benedict appears as the providential instrument of regeneration. After experiences gained in the schools of Rome, in his cave amid the solitudes of Subiaco, and as ruler of the monks of Vicovaro, he gathered round him at Subiaco a body of monks whom he distributed in twelve separate colonies and ruled for eighteen years. It was here, probably, that he conceived the lines of his celebrated monastic code, which he compiled finally when, about the year 528, he removed to the spot where now stands the renowned sanctuary of Monte Cassino. He died, according to the tradition of the Benedictine Order, on March 21, 543 A.D.

THE SPIRIT OF MONASTICISM

To understand the position of the Rule set forth by St. Benedict, and to comprehend the reason of its success in the Western world generally, it is necessary to know the meaning of monasticism in the early ages of the Church. In comparatively modern times various religious Orders have come into existence in order to meet some accidental needs of the Church, using the religious life as a means to carry out those objects. In the early ages the conception of utility or purpose, other than the perfecting of the individual soul, does not appear to have entered into the ideal of the regular life. It was regarded merely as a systematized form of life on the lines of the Gospel counsels of perfection, to be lived for its own sake and as the full expression of the Church's true and perfect life. Whatever the means, the end to be attained by religious life was the same in all systems or methods of life, namely, the more complete realization of the supernatural end of human existence, and the closer conscious union of the soul with God. This was to be attained by the removal of every hindrance to this elevation of mind, arising from self or external things; and by the practice of the Christian virtues according to the counsels of perfection. Whatever might conduce to the realization of the supernatural and higher life was enjoined and eagerly adopted. To some the practice of a solitary life in the desert appeared the most efficacious means of attaining to this desired elevation of the soul; to others the discipline of severe and sustained bodily labour seemed necessary; to others, again, the practice of astonishing austerities, of self-inflicted punishment, or of long and ever-increasing vocal prayers, seemed the most sure road by which to reach the object in view. In Egypt and the East generally the most characteristic features of the monastic life have been described as "the craving for austerities, individualism and the love of the eremitical life."

The early conception of what was necessary for monastic life was modified to some extent by St. Basil in the latter half of the fourth century. His changes tended to the introduction of community as opposed to the eremitical life and the placing of religious and ascetical exercises under the control of a Superior. From Egyptian monachism was introduced into Rome and Italy, and is found already established in Gaul about the time when St. Basil was modifying earlier practices in the East. It is somewhat difficult to say how far the individual rules of Eastern monastic reformers, like St. Basil or St. Pachomius, affected the life of Italian or other European monasteries. That these rules were known is certain, both because Rufinus had translated into Latin that of St. Basil, and St. Jerome that of Pachomius, and because St. Benedict refers in his code to "the Rule of our Holy Father Basil," as well as to the Collations of Cassian and the Lives of the Fathers of the Desert (cap. 73). But those who have best reason to pass a judgment on the matter consider that the influence of the "reforms" of St.Basil, etc., on Western monasteries had been very slight up to the time of St. Benedict, and that, at most, some of the "rules and regulations" had been borrowed in a spirit of eclecticism from the codes of Basil and Pachomius. It seems almost certain, writes a modern authority, that "in Italy, as in Gaul and Ireland, early monachism was thoroughly Egyptian in its ideals and its working."

THE WORK OF ST. BENEDICT

The danger of adopting Eastern ideals by Westerns is obvious. A method of life which may suit the people of Egypt and the East generally, may and probably will be found to be wholly unsuitable for those of Italy and Gaul, and if unsuitable and impracticable, such a method of life must inevitably lead to laxity, and tend to become a hindrance rather than a help to attain the end for which it exists. This was a recognized fact even before the time of St. Benedict. Cassian found it necessary to introduce mitigations into the Egyptian practices to make them possible for European monks, and there is evidence at least of some laxity in the monasteries of Italy in the fifth century. In his Rule (cap. I) St. Benedict speaks with severity of the Sarabites and Gyrovagi, two classes of monks to be found as the result of the system. As the same authority, quoted above, says, "This falling away may no doubt have been largely due to the fact that the monks of Italy and Gaul were trying to live up to an ideal which the climatic and other conditions of the country rendered impossible, or, at any rate, extremely difficult, and to the discouragement and demoralization consequent on an abiding sense of failure."

It was to meet this real danger that St. Benedict wrote his Rule. It must be remembered, he had had for three years at Vicovaro personal experience of the existing quasi-Eastern monastic system which had almost ended in the tragedy of his death for endeavouring to insist upon the proper carrying out of the rule which the monks professed to follow. His remedy for the state of general laxity which prevailed amongst those professing to lead the higher life was bold and novel. He did not endeavour to insist upon the discarded austerities and penitential exercises of the East, but sought reformation on new lines. He secured the old ideals of the ascetical life by moderation and common-sense ruling over men given to prayer and labour directed and controlled by obedience to authority. But the life was made possible by sufficient food, ample sleep, proper clothing, regulated prayers, and even personal austerities checked by the will of the abbot. All this was strangely different from the type of monastic observance which had hitherto prevailed not only in the East, but in Italy and Gaul. The ideals, the attainment of those spiritual heights which the soul was competent to gain, were the same, but for the more sure success Benedict's code of laws was characterized by a wide and wise discretion. To secure this end, those who wished to walk in the path of the Gospel counsels were required, as the Prologue of his Rule tells us, to promise a life-long obedience. This was a new feature, and was the first introduction of a life-long "profession," or promise of obedience "according to the Rule," and it was with the utmost care made known to the monk who "wished to fight under the law" that "from that day forth it was not lawful for him to withdraw his neck from the yoke of the rule."

THE ADOPTION OF THE RULE IN THE WEST

The result of the introduction of this principle was twofold: on the one hand it established that continuity of family life known as "stability in the community," which has since become characteristic of the monastic life; and on the other it substituted for the personal will of a Superior the code of laws by which his government was to be fashioned. Further, as the Rule shows, though St. Benedict required obedience to his code of laws, he never intended to prohibit other customs and practices not at variance with it. In fact, he expressly refers his followers to the Rule of St. Basil and to other authorities for further guidance. That in process of time St. Benedict's legislation should have superseded all others was in the nature of things inevitable. As I have elsewhere said, "The difference of tone and form between his Rule and that of others is unmistakable; and however deep and intense the piety which breathes in the *Regula Cœnobialis*, which goes under the name of St. Columban, it is a relief to pass from its crude expositions of monastic discipline to the grave and noble laws of the Roman monk. Under these circumstances it is not wonderful that by the end of the eighth century not merely had St. Benedict's Rule superseded all others, but in France the memory of any other code had so completely perished that it could be gravely doubted whether monks of any kind had existed before the time of this great monastic legislator, and whether there could be any other monks but Benedictines."

THE CONTENTS OF THE RULE

The code of monastic laws, as will be seen in the translation here printed, consists of a Prologue or Preface and seventy-three chapters. The Prologue contains many important principles of the spiritual life, and the beginning makes it clear that St. Benedict had before him the Latin translation of St. Basil's *Admonitio ad filium spiritualem.* The ideas, and many of the actual words of the introductory paragraph are evidently taken from these writings of one whom he calls "our Holy Father

Basil." In the first chapter of the Rule the "Patriarch of Western monachism" divides those wishing to lead the "higher life" into hermits or anchorites, that is, solitaries, and cœnobites, or those living together in communities. It is for this latter class only that his Rule is intended, namely, for monks living together in a monastery under an abbot and following a common form of life. Of the actual material buildings we have unfortunately very few details. All that we gather is that they were intended to be placed in the midst of fields, to be enclosed by walls, and ought to contain as far as possible all that the monks could need for their life. The monastery was to be looked on as the "school of divine service" and the "workshop" where the monk was to labour at the *artes spirituales*—the spiritual work of his supernatural vocation—by exercising himself in the use of the "Instruments of good works," described in the fourth chapter, which included the commandments of God and the natural virtues. St. Benedict shows himself as above all things practical in his system of spirituality, and he warns his followers that the first work on the road of perfection is the rooting up of their vices and labouring at the exact performance of what God long ago ordered as necessary in the ten commandments for all classes of Christians in common.

According to the Rule the monks were to be occupied in manual labour, reading and, above all, in the liturgy of the Church. The former included not merely labour in the fields, but the exercise of any art in which some might be proficient, the result of which might be sold for the benefit of the monastery, or be in any other way useful for the common good. The necessity of supplying books for public and private reading would show that St. Benedict, although he does not expressly mention it, intended monks that were capable of writing and illuminating to be employed in this way, which subsequently proved of the greatest service to European civilization by multiplying in the *scriptoria* of the monastic houses, and thus preserving to our times the literature of classical ages and the works of the early Fathers of the Christian Church. The time devoted to reading—to intellectual studies generally—varied according to the period of the year, but the hours after Vespers, from three to six o'clock, as well as Sundays, were apparently set apart for study (chap. 48); whilst St. Benedict's declaration that every monk must have his *graphium* or style, and his tablets for writing, shows that intellectual work was contemplated by him. The centre of the monastic life, according to the Rule, was unquestionably the Liturgy, or as St. Benedict calls it, the *Opus Dei,* or Divine Office. "Nothing was to be preferred" to this part of the common life of the religious house, and the legislator devotes several chapters of his code to ordering and arranging the Psalmody for his monks.

The monastery properly constituted resembled a self-centred state or city. Surrounded by walls, with its workshops, its farms, its gardens, its mill, etc., it was governed by the various necessary officials under the direction of a Superior. St. Benedict, however, conceived the religious house to resemble rather the family of which the abbot held the place of the father, and a father in whom the members of the family acknowledged, with affectionate respect, the obedience due to our Lord Himself, because, as he says, "he occupies the place of Christ." This father, or abbot, was chosen by the votes of the monks, and the principles which should guide him in ruling his family are amongst the most important and useful laid down by St. Benedict. Though he has the appointment of his officials, and has the right and duty of ruling and watching over each individual member of the religious community, he himself is subject to the provisions of the Rule, and is bound to live the common life of the brethren.

THE TEXT OF THE RULE

It is unnecessary to say much under the present circumstances as to the text of the Rule of St. Benedict. There appears never to have been any serious doubt cast upon the fact that the book as we have it now is substantially what came from the pen of the author. In the text of a work so frequently copied as this must have been during the whole of the Middle Ages, and especially in the period from the ninth to the twelfth century, when it was practically the only monastic Rule of the West, it is inevitable that differences should be found to exist. The original, or what was believed to have been the original autograph of

St. Benedict, after having been long preserved at Monte
Cassino perished in a disastrous fire in the Monastery of Teano,
whither it had been taken for safety during the invasion of the
Saracens into Italy. It is of interest to Englishmen to know that
the oldest MS. at present known is Hatton MS. 42, written in
England in the seventh or eighth century; the next oldest being
the St. Gall MS., which is probably not older than the beginning
of the ninth century. For the benefit of nuns in England who followed the Rule, and of others, the work was several times translated into English during the Middle Ages, and for the benefit
of the "devout religious women" of his diocese it was
"Englished" by Bishop Richard Foxe, and printed by Pynson on
January 22, 1516–17. In the seventeenth century another translation was made partly by Father Leander Jones and partly by
Father Cuthbert Fursden in their connection with the English
Benedictine nuns of Cambrai. This was published first in 1638,
and has been more than once since printed. Upon this the present translation has been based, although it must be confessed
that I have found it necessary to take considerable liberties with
the work of the seventeenth-century translators.

The Prologue

Listen my son, and turn the ear of thine heart to the precepts of thy Master.[1] Receive readily, and faithfully carry out the advice of a loving Father, so that by the work of obedience you may return to Him, whom you have left by the sloth of disobedience. For thee, therefore, whosoever thou be, my words are intended, who, giving up thy own will, dost take the all-powerful and excellent arms of obedience to fight under the Lord Christ, the true King.

First, beg of Him with most earnest prayer to finish the good work begun; that He who now hath deigned to count us among His children may never be grieved by our evil deeds. For at all times we must so serve Him with the good things He has given us, that He may not, as an angry Father, disinherit His children, nor as a dread Lord, provoked by our evil deeds, deliver us to everlasting punishment as wicked servants who refuse to follow Him to glory.

Let us, therefore, arise at once, the Scripture stirring us up, saying, *It is now the hour for us to rise from sleep.*[2] And, our eyes now open to the divine light, let us with wondering ears hearken to the divine voice, daily calling to us and warning us, *To-day if you shall hear His voice, harden not your hearts;*[3] and again, *He that hath ears, let him hear what the Spirits saith to the Churches.*[4] And what does He say? *Come, ye children, and hearken unto Me: I will teach you the fear of the Lord.*[5] *Run while ye have the light of life, that the darkness of death overtake ye not.*[6]

1

And our Lord, seeking His workman among the multitude of those to whom He thus speaks, says again, *Who is the man that will have life, and desireth to see good days?*[7] And if thou, hearing this, reply, "I am he": God says to you, If thou desirest to possess true and everlasting life *restrain thy tongue from evil, and thy lips that they speak no guile. Decline from evil and do good; seek after peace and pursue it.*[8] And when you have done this My eyes shall be on you, and My ears shall be open to your prayers. And before you can call upon Me, I will say to you, *Behold, I am present.*[9] What can be more agreeable, dearest brethren, than this voice of our Lord inviting us? Behold how in His loving kindness He shows us the way of life!

Therefore, with our loins girt by faith, and by the practice of good works under the guidance of His Gospel, let us walk in the path He has marked out for us, that we may deserve to see Him who has called us in His kingdom.[10]

If we would live in the shelter of this kingdom, we can reach it only by speeding on the way of good works (by this path alone is it to be attained). But let us, with the prophet, ask our Lord, and say to Him, *Lord, who shall dwell in Thy tabernacle? or who shall rest on Thy holy hill?*[11] And when we have so asked, let us her our Lord's answer, pointing out to us the way to this His dwelling, and saying, *He that walketh without spot and worketh justice: he that speaketh truth in his heart: that hath not forged guile with his tongue: he that hath not done evil to his neighbour, and hath not taken up reproach against him.*[12] He that, casting out of the inmost thoughts of his heart the suggestions of the evil-minded devil trying to lead him astray, has brought them all to naught: he that taking hold of his thoughts whilst in their birth hath dashed them against the rock, which is Christ. They who, fearing the Lord, are not lifted up by their good observance, but knowing that all that is good in them comes not from themselves but from the Lord, extol His work in them, saying with the prophet, *Not to us, O Lord, not to us, but to Thy Name give glory.*[13] Thus the Apostle Paul imputed nothing of his preaching to himself, saying, *By the grace of God I am what I am.*[14] And again he saith, *He that glorieth, let him glory in the Lord.*[15]

Hence also our Lord in the Gospel says, *He that heareth these My words and doth them, I will liken him to a wise man that hath built his house upon a rock. The floods came, the winds blew and beat against that house, and it fell not, because it was founded upon a rock.*[16.] In fulfilment whereof our Lord daily looketh for deeds in us complying with His holy admonitions. Therefore are the days of this our life lengthened for awhile for the mending of our evil deeds, according to the words of the apostle, *Knowest thou not that the patience of God leadeth thee to repentance?*[17] For our loving Lord says, *I will not the death of the sinner, but that he be converted and live.*[18]

So questioning the Lord, brethren, we have heard on what conditions we may dwell in His temple; and if we fulfil these we shall be heirs of the kingdom of heaven. Therefore must our hearts and bodies be prepared to fight under the holy obedience of His commands, and we must beg our Lord to supply by the help of His grace what by nature is not possible to us. And if, fleeing from the pains of hell, we will to attain to life everlasting, we must, whilst time yet serves and whilst we live in the flesh and the light is still on our path, hasten to do now what will profit us for all eternity.

We are therefore now about to institute a school for the service of God, in which we hope nothing harsh nor nor burdensome will be ordained. But if we proceed in certain things with some little severity, sound reason so advising for the amendment of vices or the preserving of charity, do not for fear of this forthwith flee from the way of salvation, which is always narrow in the beginning.[19] In living our life, however, and by the growth of faith, when the heart has been enlarged, the path of God's commandments is run with unspeakable loving sweetness; so that never leaving His school, but persevering in the monastery until death in His teaching, we share by our patience in the sufferings of Christ, and so merit to be partakers of His kingdom.[20]

Chapter I

Of the Several Kinds of Monks and Their Lives

It is recognized that there are four kinds of monks. The first are the Cenobites: that is, those who live in a monastery under a Rule or an abbot. The second kind is that of Anchorites, or

Hermits, who not in the first fervour of conversion, but after long trial in the monastery, and already taught by the example of many others, have learnt to fight against the devil, are well prepared to go forth from the ranks of the brotherhood to the single combat of the desert. They can now, by God's help, safely fight against the vices of their flesh and against evil thoughts singly, with their own hand and arm and without the encouragement of a companion. The third and worst kind of monks is that of the Sarabites, who have not been tried under any Rule nor schooled by an experienced master, as gold is proved in the furnace, but soft as is lead and still in their works cleaving to the world, are known to lie to God by their tonsure.

These in twos or threes, or more frequently singly, are shut up, without a shepherd; not in the Lord's fold, but in their own. The pleasure of carrying out their particular desires is their law, and whatever they dream of or choose this they call holy; but what they like not, that they account unlawful.

The fourth class of monks is called Gyrovagi (or Wanderers). These move about all their lives through various countries, staying as guests for three or four days at different monasteries. They are always on the move and never settle down, and are slaves to their own wills and to the enticements of gluttony. In every way they are worse than the Sarabites, and of their wretched way of life it is better to be silent than to speak.

Leaving these therefore aside, let us by God's help set down a Rule for Cenobites, who are the best kind of monks.[21]

Chapter II

What the Abbot Should Be

An abbot to be fit to rule a monastery should ever remember what he is called, and in his acts illustrate his high calling. For in a monastery he is considered to take the place of Christ, since he is called by His name as the apostle saith, *Ye have received the spirit of the adoption of sons, whereby we cry, Abba, Father.*[22] Therefore the abbot should neither teach, ordain, nor require anything against the command of our Lord

(God forbid!), but in the minds of his disciples let his orders and teaching be mingled with the leaven of divine justice.

The abbot should ever be mindful that at the dread judgment of God there will be inquiry both as to his teaching and as to the obedience of his disciples. Let the abbot know that any lack of goodness, which the master of the family shall find in his flock, will be accounted the shepherd's fault. On the other hand, he shall be acquitted in so far as he shall have shown all the watchfulness of a shepherd over a restless and disobedient flock: and if as their pastor he shall have employed every care to cure their corrupt manners, he shall be declared guiltless in the Lord's judgment, and he may say with the prophet, *I have not hidden Thy justice in my heart; I have told Thy truth and Thy salvation;*[23] *but they contemned and despised me.*[24] And then in the end shall death be inflicted as a meet punishment upon the sheep which have not responded to his care. When, therefore, any one shall receive the name of abbot, he ought to rule his disciples with a twofold teaching: that is, he should first show them in deeds rather than words all that is good and holy. To such as are understanding, indeed, he may expound the Lord's behests by words; but to the hard-hearted and to the simple-minded he must manifest the divine precepts in his life. Thus, what he has taught his disciples to be contrary to God's law, let him show in his own deeds that such things are not to be done, lest preaching to others *he himself become a castaway,*[25] and God say unto him thus sinning, *Why dost thou declare My justices, and take My testament in thy mouth? Thou hast hated discipline, and cast My speeches behind thee.*[26] And *Thou, who didst see the mote in thy brother's eye, hast thou not seen the beam that is in thine own?*[27]

Let him make no distinction of persons in the monastery. Let not one be loved more than another, save such as be found to excel in obedience or good works. Let not the free-born be put before the serf-born in religion, unless there be other reasonable cause for it. If upon due consideration the abbot shall see such cause he may place him where he pleases; otherwise let all keep their own places, because *whether bond or free we are all one in Christ,*[28] and bear an equal burden of service under one Lord: *for with God there is no accepting of persons.*[29] For one thing only are we preferred by Him, if we are found better than others in good works and more humble. Let the abbot therefore have equal love for all, and let all, according to their deserts, be under the same discipline.

The abbot in his teaching should always observe that apostolic rule which saith, *Reprove, entreat, rebuke.*[30] That is to say, as occasions require he ought to mingle encouragement with reproofs. Let him manifest the sternness of a master and the loving affection of a father. He must reprove the undisciplined and restless severely, but he should exhort such as are obedient, quiet and patient, for their better profit. We charge him, however, to reprove and punish the stubborn and negligent. Let him not shut his eyes to the sins of offenders; but, directly they begin to show themselves and to grow, he must use every means to root them up utterly, remembering the fate of Heli, the priest of Silo.[31] To the more virtuous and apprehensive, indeed, he may for the first or second time use words of warning; but in dealing with the stubborn, the hard-hearted, the proud and the disobedient, even at the very beginning of their sin, let him chastise them with stripes and with bodily punishment, knowing that it is written, *The fool is not corrected with words.*[32] And again, *Strike thy son with a rod and thou shalt deliver his soul from death.*[33]

The abbot ought ever to bear in mind what he is and what he is called; he ought to know that to whom more is entrusted, from him more is exacted. Let him recognize how difficult and how hard a task he has undertaken, to rule souls and to make himself a servant to the humours of many. One, forsooth, must be led by gentle words, another by sharp reprehension, another by persuasion; and thus shall he so shape and adapt himself to the character and intelligence of each, that he not only suffer no loss in the flock entrusted to his care, but may even rejoice in its good growth. Above all things let him not slight nor make little of the souls committed to his care, heeding more fleeting, worldly and frivolous things; but let him remember always that he has undertaken the government of souls, of which he shall also have to give an account. And that he may not complain of the want of temporal means, let him remember that it is written, *Seek first the kingdom of God, and His justice, and all things shall be given to you.*[34] And again, *Nothing is wanting to such as fear Him.*[35]

He should know that whoever undertakes the government of

souls must prepare himself to account for them. And however great the number of the brethren under him may be, let him understand for certain that at the Day of Judgment he will have to give to our Lord an account of all their souls as well as of his own. In this way, by fearing the inquiry concerning his flock which the Shepherd will hold, he is solicitous on account of others' souls as well as of his own, and thus whilst reclaiming other men by his corrections, he frees himself also from all vice.

Chapter III

On Taking Counsel of the Brethren

Whenever any weighty matters have to be transacted in the monastery let the abbot call together all the community and himself propose the matter for discussion. After hearing the advice of the brethren let him consider it in his own mind, and then do what he shall judge most expedient. We ordain that all must be called to council, because the Lord often reveals to a younger member what is best. And let the brethren give their advice with all humble subjection, and presume not stiffly to defend their own opinion. Let them rather leave the matter to the abbot's discretion, so that all submit to what he shall deem best. As it becometh disciples to obey their master, so doth it behove the master to dispose of all things with forethought and justice.

In all things, therefore, every one shall follow the Rule as their master, and let no one rashly depart from it. In the monastery no one is to be led by the desires of his own heart, neither shall any one within or without the monastery presume to argue wantonly with his abbot. If he presume to do so let him be subjected to punishment according to the Rule.

The abbot, however, must himself do all things in the fear of God and according to the Rule, knowing that he shall undoubtedly have to give an account of his whole government to God the most just Judge.

If anything of less moment has to be done in the monastery let the abbot take advice of the seniors only, as it is written, *Do all things with counsel, and thou shalt not afterwards repent of it.*[36]

Chapter IV

The Instruments of Good Works

First of all, to love the Lord God with all our heart, with all our soul, with all our strength.[37]

2. Then, to love our neighbour as ourself.[38]
3. Then, not to kill.[39]
4. Not to commit adultery.[40]
5. Not to steal.[41]
6. Not to be covetous.[42]
7. Not to bear false witness.[43]
8. To respect all men.[44]
9. Not to do to another what one would not have done to oneself.[45]
10. To deny oneself in order to follow Christ.[46]
11. To chastise the body.[47]
12. Not to be fond of pleasures.[48]
13. To love fasting.[49]
14. To give refreshment to the poor.[50]
15. To clothe the naked.[51]
16. To visit the sick.[52]
17. To bury the dead.[53]
18. To come to the help of those in trouble.[54]
19. To comfort those in sadness.[55]
20. To become a stranger to the ways of the world.[56]
21. To prefer nothing to the love of Christ.[57]
22. Not to give way to wrath.[58]
23. Not to harbour anger for any time.[59]
24. Not to foster deceit in the heart.[60]
25. Not to make a false peace.[61]
26. Not to depart from charity.[62]
27. Not to swear at all, lest one forswears.[63]
28. To speak the truth with heart and lips.[64]
29. Not to return evil for evil.[65]
30. Not to do an injury, but patiently to suffer one when done.[66]
31. To love one's enemies.[67]
32. Not to speak ill of those who speak ill of one, but rather to speak well of them.[68]

33. To suffer persecution for justice sake.[69]
34. Not to be proud.[70]
35. Not to be a winebibber.[71]
36. Not to be a great eater.[72]
37. Not to be given to sleep.[73]
38. Not to be slothful.[74]
39. Not to be a murmurer.[75]
40. Not to be a detractor.[76]
41. To put one's trust in God.[77]
42. When one sees any good in oneself to attribute it to God, not to oneself.[78]
43. That a man recognize that it is he who does evil, and so let him attribute it to himself.[79]
44. To fear the day of judgment.[80]
45. To be afraid of hell.[81]
46. To desire life everlasting with entire spiritual longing.[82]
47. To have the vision of death before one's eyes daily.[83]
48. To watch over the actions of one's life every hour of the day.[84]
49. To know for certain that God sees one everywhere.[85]
50. To dash at once against Christ (as against a rock) evil thoughts which rise up in the mind.[86]
51. And to reveal all such to one's spiritual Father.[87]
52. To guard one's lips from uttering evil or wicked words.[88]
53. Not to be fond of much talking.[89]
54. Not to speak idle words, or such as move to laughter.[90]
55. Not to love much or boisterous laughter.[91]
56. Willingly to hear holy reading.[92]
57. Often to devote oneself to prayer.[93]
58. Daily with tears and sighs to confess to God in prayer one's past offences, and to avoid them for the future.[94]
59. Not to give way to the desires of the flesh:[95] and to hate one's own will.[96]
60. In all things to obey the abbot's commands, even though he himself (which God forbid) should act otherwise, remembering our Lord's precept, *What they say, do ye, but what they do, do ye not.*[97]
61. Not to wish to be called holy before one is so; but to be holy first so as to be called such with truth.[98]

62. Daily in one's acts to keep God's commandments.[99]
63. To love chastity.[100]
64. To hate no man.[101]
65. Not to be jealous or envious.[102]
66. Not to love wrangling.[103]
67. To show no arrogant spirit.[104]
68. To reverence the old.[105]
69. To love the young.[106]
70. To pray for one's enemies for the love of Christ.[107]
71. To make peace with an adversary before the sun sets.[108]
72. And, never to despair of God's mercy.[109]

Behold these are the tools of our spiritual craft; when we shall have made use of them constantly day and night, and shall have proved them at the day of judgment, that reward shall be given us by our Lord, which He has promised, *Which eye hath not seen, nor ear heard, nor hath it entered into the heart of man to conceive what God hath prepared for those that love Him.*[110] Steadfastly abiding in the community, the workshop where all these instruments are made use of is the cloister of the monastery.

Chapter V

On Obedience

The first degree of humility is prompt obedience. This is required of all who, whether by reason of the holy servitude to which they are pledged, or through fear of hell, or to attain to the glory of eternal life, hold nothing more dear than Christ. Such disciples delay not in doing what is ordered by their superior, just as if the command had come from God. Of such our Lord says, *At the hearing of the ear he hath obeyed me.*[111] And to the teachers He likewise says, *He that heareth you, heareth me.*[113]

For this reason such disciples, surrendering forthwith all they possess, and giving up their own will, leave unfinished what they were working at, and with the ready foot of obedience in their acts follow the word of command. Thus, as it were, at the same moment comes the order of the master and the finished work of the disciple: with the speed of the fear of God both go jointly forward and are quickly effected by such as ardently desire to walk in the way of eternal life. These take the narrow way, of which the Lord saith, *Narrow is the way which leads to life.*[113] That is, they live not as they themselves will, neither do they obey their own desires and pleasures; but following the command and direction of another and abiding in their monasteries, their desire is to be ruled by an abbot. Without doubt such as these carry out that saying of our Lord, *I came not to do my own will, but the will of Him Who sent me.*[114]

This kind of obedience will be both acceptable to God and pleasing to men, when what is ordered is not done out of fear, or slowly and coldly, grudgingly, or with reluctant protest. Obedience shown to superiors is indeed given to God, Who Himself hath said, *He that heareth you, heareth Me.*[115] What is commanded should be done by those under obedience, with a good will, since *God loveth a cheerful giver.*[116] If the disciple obey unwillingly and murmur in word as well as in heart, it will not be accepted by God, Who considereth the heart of a murmurer, even if he do what was ordered. For a work done in this spirit shall have no reward; rather shall the doer incur the penalty appointed for murmurers if he amend not and make not satisfaction.

Chapter VI

On Silence

L et us do as the prophet says, *I have said, I will keep my ways, that I offend not with my tongue. I have been watchful over my mouth: I held my peace and humbled myself and was silent from speaking even good things.*[117] Here the prophet shows that, for the sake of silence, we are at times to abstain even from good talk. If this be so, how much more needful is it that we refrain from evil words, on account of the penalty of the sin! Because of the importance of silence, therefore, let leave to speak be seldom given, even to perfect disciples, although their talk be of good and holy matters and tending to edification, since it is written, *In much speaking, thou shalt not escape sin.*[118] The master, indeed, should speak and teach: the disciple should hold his peace and listen.

Whatever, therefore, has to be asked of the prior, let it be done with all humility and with reverent submission. But as to coarse, idle words, or such as move to laughter, we utterly condemn and ban them in all places. We do not allow any disciple to give mouth to them.

Chapter VII

On Humility

B rethren, Holy Scripture cries out to us, saying, *Every one who exalteth himself shall be humbled, and he who humbleth himself shall be exalted.*[119] In this it tells us that every form of self-exaltation is a kind of pride, which the prophet declares he carefully avoided, where he says, *Lord, my heart is not exalted, neither are my eyes lifted up; neither have I walked in great things, nor in wonders above myself.* And why? *If I did not think humbly, but exalted my soul: as a child weaned from his mother, so wilt Thou reward my soul.*[120]

Wherefore, brethren, if we would scale the summit of humility, and swiftly gain the heavenly height which is reached by our lowliness in this present life, we must set up a ladder of climbing deeds like that which Jacob saw in his dream, whereon angels were descending and ascending. Without doubt that descending and ascending is to be understood by us as signifying that we descend by exalting ourselves and ascend by humbling ourselves. But the ladder itself thus set up is our life in this world, which by humility of heart is lifted by our Lord to heaven. Our body and soul we may indeed call the sides of the ladder in which our divine vocation has set the divers steps of humility and discipline we have to ascend.

The first step of humility, then, is reached when a man, with the fear of God always before his eyes, does not allow himself to forget, but is ever mindful of all God's commandments. He remembers, moreover, that such as contemn God fall into hell for their sins, and that life eternal awaits such as fear Him. And warding off at each moment all sin and defect in thought and word, of eye, hand or foot, of self-will, let such a one bestir himself to prune away the lusts of the flesh.

Let him think that he is seen at all times by God from heaven; and that wheresoever he may be, all his actions are visible to the eye of God and at all times are reported by the angels. The prophet shows us this when he says that God is ever present to our thoughts: *God searcheth the hearts and reins.*[121] And again, *The Lord knoweth the thoughts of men that they are vain.*[122] He also saith, *Thou hast understood my thoughts afar off;*[123] and again, *The thought of man shall confess Thee.*[124] In order, then, that the humble brother may be careful to avoid wrong thoughts let him always say in his heart, *Then shall I be without spot before Him, if I shall keep me from my iniquity.*[125]

We are forbidden to do our own will, since Scripture tells us, *Leave thy own will and desire.*[126] And again, *We beg of God in prayer that His will may be done in us.*[127]

Rightly are we taught therefore not to do our own will, if we take heed of what the Scripture teaches: *There are ways which to men seem right, the end whereof plungeth even into the deep pit of hell.*[128] And again, when we fear what is said about the negligent, *They are corrupted, and made abominable in their pleasures.*[129] But in regard of the desires of the flesh we ought to believe that God is present with us; as the prophet says, speaking to the Lord, *O Lord, all my desire is before Thee.*[130]

We have therefore to beware of evil desires, since death stands close at the door of pleasure. It is for this reason that Scripture bids us, *Follow not thy concupiscences.*[131] If, therefore, the eyes of the Lord behold both the good and the bad; if He be ever looking down from heaven upon the sons of men to find one who thinks of God or seeks Him; and if day and night what we do is made known to Him—for these reasons, by the angels appointed to watch over us, we should always take heed, brethren, lest God may sometime or other see us, as the prophet says in the Psalm, *inclined to evil and become unprofitable servants.*[132] Even though He spare us for a time, because He is loving and waits for our conversion to better ways, let us fear that He may say to us hereafter, *These things thou hast done and I held my peace.*[133]

The second step of humility is reached when any one not loving self-will takes no heed to satisfy his own desires, but copies in his life what our Lord said, *I came not to do My own will, but the will of Him Who sent Me.*[134] Scripture likewise proclaims that self-will engendereth punishment, and necessity purchaseth a crown.

The third step of humility is reached when a man, for the love of God, submits himself with all obedience to a superior, imitating our Lord, of whom the apostle saith, *He was made obedient even unto death.*[135.]

The fourth step of humility is reached when any one in the exercise of his obedience patiently and with a quiet mind bears all that is inflicted on him, things contrary to nature, and even at times unjust, and in suffering all these he neither wearies nor gives over the work, since the Scripture says, *He only that persevereth to the end shall be saved;*[136] also *Let thy heart be comforted, and expect the Lord.*[137] And in order to show that for our Lord's sake the faithful man ought to bear all things, no matter how contrary to nature they may be (the psalmist), in the person of the sufferers, says, *For thee we suffer death all the day long; we are esteemed as sheep for the slaughter.*[138] Secure in the hope of divine reward they rejoice, saying, *But in all things we overcome by the help of Him Who hath loved us.*[139]

Elsewhere also Scripture says, *Thou hast proved us, O Lord; Thou hast tried us, as silver is tried, with fire. Thou hast brought us into the snare; Thou hast laid tribulation upon our backs.*[140] And to show that we ought to be subject to a prior (or superior) it goes on, *Thou has placed men over our heads.*[141] And, moreover, they fulfil the Lord's command by patience in adversity and injury, who, *when struck on one cheek, offer the other;* when one *taketh away their coat leave go their cloak also,* and who being compelled to carry a burden one mile, go two; who, with

Paul the apostle, suffer false brethren, and bless those who speak ill of them.[142]

The fifth step of humility is reached when a monk manifests to his abbot, by humble confession, all the evil thoughts of his heart and his secret faults. The Scripture urges us to do this where it says, *Reveal thy way to the Lord and hope in Him.*[143] It also says, *Confess to the Lord, because he is good, because His mercy endureth for ever.*[144] And the prophet also says, *I have made known unto Thee mine offence, and mine injustices I have not hidden. I have said, I will declare openly against myself mine injustices to the Lord; and Thou hast pardoned the wickedness of my heart.*[145]

The sixth step of humility is reached when a monk is content with all that is mean and vile; and in regard to everything enjoined him accounts himself a poor and worthless workman, saying with the prophet, *I have been brought to nothing, and knew it not. I have become as a beast before Thee, and I am always with Thee.*[146]

The seventh step of humility is reached when a man not only confesses with his tongue that he is most lowly and inferior to others, but in his inmost heart believes so. Such a one, humbling himself, exclaims with the prophet, *I am a worm and no man, the reproach of men and the outcast of the people.*[147] *I have been exalted and am humbled and confounded.*[148] And again, *It is good for me that Thou hast humbled me, that I may learn Thy commandments.*[149]

The eighth step of humility is reached when a monk does nothing but what the common rule of the monastery, or the example of his seniors, enforces.

The ninth step of humility is reached when a monk restrains his tongue from talking, and, practising silence, speaks not till a question be asked him, since Scripture says, *In many words thou shalt not avoid sin,*[150] and *a talkative man shall not be directed upon the earth.*[151]

The tenth step of humility is attained to when one is not easily and quickly moved to laughter, for it is written, *The fool lifteth his voice in laughter.*[152]

The eleventh step of humility is reached when a monk, in speaking, do so quietly and without laughter, humbly, gravely and in a few words and not with a loud voice, for it is written, *A wise man is known by a few words.*[153]

The twelfth step of humility is reached when a monk not only has humility in his heart, but even shows it also exteriorly to all who behold him. Thus, whether he be in the oratory at the "Work of God," in the monastery, or in the garden, on a journey, or in the fields, or wheresoever he be, sitting, standing or walking, always let him, with head bent and eyes fixed on the ground, bethink himself of his sins and imagine that he is arraigned before the dread judgment of God. Let him be ever saying to himself, with the publican in the Gospel, *Lord, I a sinner am not worthy to lift mine eyes to heaven;*[154] and with the prophet, *I am bowed down and humbled on every side.*[155]

When all these steps of humility have been mounted the monk will presently attain to that love of God which is perfect and casteth out fear. By means of this love everything which before he had observed not without fear, he shall now begin to do by habit, without any trouble and, as it were, naturally. He acts now not through fear of hell, but for the love of Christ, out of a good habit and a delight in virtue. All this our Lord will vouchsafe to work by the Holy Ghost in His servant, now cleansed from vice and sin.

Chapter VIII

Of the Divine Office at Night Time

In the winter time—that is, from the first of November till Easter—the brethren shall get up at the eighth hour of the night by reasonable calculation, so that having rested till a little after midnight they may rise refreshed. Let the time that remains after Matins be used, by those brethren who need it, for the study of the Psalter or lessons. From Easter to the foresaid first of November let the hour for saying Matins be so arranged that after a brief interval, during which the brethren may go forth for the necessities of nature, Lauds, which are to be said at daybreak, may presently follow.

Chapter IX

How Many Psalms are to be Said in the Night Hours

In the winter season, having first said the verse, *O God, incline unto mine aid; O Lord, make haste to help me,*[156] the words, *O Lord, Thou shalt open my lips and my mouth shall declare Thy praise*[157] are then to be said thrice. After this the third Psalm is to be said with a *Gloria;* after which the ninety-fourth Psalm, with an antiphon, is to be recited or sung, followed by a hymn, and then six psalms with their antiphons. When these are ended and a versicle said, let the abbot give a blessing; and then, all being seated, let three lessons from the book placed on the lectern be read by the brethren in turns. Between these lessons three responsories are to be sung, two without a *Gloria.* After that third lesson, however, let the cantor add the *Gloria* to the responsory, and as soon as he begins it let all rise from their seats out of honour and reverence to the Holy Trinity.

Let the divinely inspired books of the Old and New Testament be read at Matins, together with their expositions from the best known, orthodox and Catholic Fathers.

After these three lessons, with their responsories, let six other psalms be sung with the *Alleluia.* A lesson from the Apostle is then to be said by heart, and a verse with the petition of the Litany—that is, *Kyrie eleison*—and so let the night watches (or Matins) end.

Chapter X

How Matins, or the Night Praises, are to be Said in the Summer Season

From Easter to the first day of November the same number of psalms as above appointed are to be said. On account of the short nights, however, the lessons are not to be read from the book, but in place of the three lessons let one out of the Old Testament be said by heart and followed by a short responsory.

Let all the rest be done as we have arranged above, so that, without counting the third and ninety-fourth Psalm, there may never be less than twelve psalms at Matins.

Chapter XI

How Matins, or the Night Watches, are to be Celebrated on Sundays

On Sunday let the brethren rise earlier for Matins, in which the following order is to be observed: when six psalms and the versicle have been sung, as we have before arranged, let all sit down in proper order and let four lessons be read from the book with their responsories, in the manner before prescribed. To the fourth responsory only let the cantor add the *Gloria,* and when he begins it let all rise at once out of reverence. After these lessons six other psalms[158] follow in order with their antiphons and a versicle as before. Then let four other lessons be read with their responsories in the same way as the former, and then three canticles out of the Prophets, appointed by the abbot: these canticles are to be sung with *Alleluia.*

When the versicle has been said, and the abbot has given the blessing, four more lessons from the New Testament are to be read, in the same order as before. After the fourth responsory let the abbot begin the hymn *Te Deum laudamus,* and when that is finished he shall read a lesson from the Gospel, with reverence and fear, whilst all stand. At the conclusion of this let all answer Amen, and let the abbot immediately go on with the hymn *Te decet laus*; after the blessing let them begin Lauds.

This method of singing Matins on Sundays is to be observed always, as well in summer as in winter, unless perchance (which God forbid) they get up late, and the lessons or responsories have to be somewhat shortened. Let great care be taken that this shall not happen; but if it does, let him to whose carelessness it is due make full satisfaction to God in the oratory.

Chapter XII

How Lauds are to be Solemnized

At Lauds on Sunday let the sixty-sixth Psalm be first said straight on and without an antiphon. After this the fiftieth is to be said with *Alleluia,* with the hundred and seventeenth and the sixty-second. Then follow the "Blessings" (or *Benedicte*) and the "Praises" (or *Laudate* psalms), a lesson from the Apocalypse, said by heart, a responsory and hymn, the versicle and the canticle from the Gospel (or *Benedictus*) with the litanies (or *Kyrie*), and so conclude.

Chapter XIII

How Lauds are to be Celebrated on Ordinary Days

On ordinary week-days let Lauds be celebrated as follows: the sixty-sixth Psalm is to be said, as on Sunday, straight on without any antiphon, and somewhat slowly, to allow of all being in their places for the fiftieth Psalm, which is to be said with an antiphon. After this come two other psalms according to custom: that is, on Monday, the fifth and thirty-fifth; on Tuesday, the forty-second and fifty-sixth; on Wednesday, the sixty-third and sixty-fourth; on Thursday, the eighty-seventh and eighty-ninth; on Friday, the seventy-fifth and ninety-first; on Saturday, the hundred and forty-second and the Canticle of Deuteronomy, which must be divided into two *Glorias.* But on other days let a canticle out of the Prophets be said, each on its proper day, according to the custom of the Roman Church. After these let the *Praises* (or *Laudate* Psalms) follow, then a lesson of the Apostle, said by heart, the responsory, hymn and versicle, the canticle from the Gospel (or *Benedictus*), the litanies (or *Kyrie eleison*), and the office is completed.

Lauds and Evensong are never to be finished without the Lord's prayer at the end. This is said by the prior (that is, the superior) aloud, so that all may hear, because of the thorns of scandal which are always cropping up: that the community, by reason of the pledge given in this prayer, in the words, *Forgive us our trespasses as we forgive them that trespass against us,* may purge themselves from this kind of vice. In saying the other Hours, however, the last part of the prayer only is said aloud that all may answer, *But deliver us from evil.*

Chapter XIV

How Matins is to be Said on the Feast Days of Saints

On Saints' feast days and on all solemnities let Matins be said in the manner we have ordered for Sunday, except that the psalms, antiphons and lessons are said which are proper to the day itself. The method of saying them, however, shall remain as before prescribed.

Chapter XV

At What Seasons Alleluia is to be Said

From the holy feast of Easter until Whitsuntide *Alleluia* is to be always said both with the psalms and in the responsories. From Whitsuntide till the beginning of Lent let it be said every night at Matins only with the last six psalms. On every Sunday out of Lent let the Canticles, Lauds, Prime, Tierce, Sext and None be said with *Alleluia,* but Evensong with antiphons. Responsories, however, except from Easter till Pentecost, are never to be said with *Alleluia.*

Chapter XVI

How the Day Divine Office is to be Said

The prophet says, *Seven times I have sung Thy praises.*[159] This sacred number of seven will be kept by us if we perform the duties of our service in the Hours of Lauds, Prime, Tierce, Sext, None, Evensong and Compline. It was of these day

Hours the prophet said, *Seven times a day I have sung Thy praises,* for of the night watches the same prophet says, *At midnight I arose to confess to Thee.*[160] At these times, therefore, let us give praise to our Creator for His just judgments, that is, at Lauds, Prime, Tierce, Sext, None, Evensong and Compline, and at night let us rise to confess to Him.

Chapter XVII

How Many Psalms are to be Said in These Hours

We have already settled the order of the psalmody for the Nocturns and for Lauds, let us now arrange for the Hours which follow. At Prime three psalms are to be said separately, that is, not under one *Gloria.* After the verse, *O God, incline unto mine aid,* and before the psalms are begun, the hymn of each Hour is to be said. At the end of the three psalms a lesson is recited, then with the versicle and *Kyrie eleison* the Hour is concluded. The Hours of Tierce, Sext and None are to be said in the same way, that is, the verse *(O God, incline, etc.),* the hymns of these Hours, three psalms, the lesson and versicle, and with *Kyrie eleison* they are concluded.

If the community be large the Hours shall be sung with antiphons, but if it be small they are to be without. Evensong shall be said with four psalms and antiphons, after which a lesson is to be recited, then a responsory, hymn, versicle, canticle from the Gospel (i.e. *Magnificat*), and it is concluded by the litanies (or *Kyrie*) and the Lord's Prayer. Compline shall consist in the saying of three psalms straight through and without antiphons, followed by the hymn of the Hour, a lesson, versicle, *Kyrie eleison*, and shall conclude with the blessing.

Chapter XVIII

The Order in Which the Psalms are to be Said

Let the verse, *O God, incline unto mine aid; O Lord, make haste to help me,* with a *Gloria,* always come first, followed by the hymn of each Hour. Then, on Sundays, at Prime, four divisions of the hundred and eighteenth Psalm are to be said; and at the other Hours of Tierce, Sext and None three divisions of the same. On Monday, at Prime, psalms first, second and third are recited, and so on each day till Sunday, three other psalms in order up to the nineteenth Psalm: the ninth and seventeenth Psalm being each divided in two by a *Gloria*. In this way the Sunday Matins may always begin with the twentieth Psalm.

On Mondays, at Tierce, Sext and None let the remaining nine divisions of the hundred and eighteenth Psalm be said, three at each Hour. The hundred and eighteenth Psalm being finished on the two days, Sunday and Monday, therefore on Tuesday, at Tierce, Sext and None the three psalms at each Hour shall be the nine from the hundred and nineteenth to the hundred and twenty-seventh. And these same psalms are to be repeated at the Hours till the Sunday. A uniform order of the hymns, lessons and versicles is to be likewise observed, so that the hundred and eighteenth Psalm is always begun on the Sunday.

Four psalms are to be sung each day at Evensong. These begin with the hundred and ninth Psalm and conclude with the hundred and forty-seventh, omitting those already set apart for the various other Hours, that is to say, from the hundred and seventeenth Psalm to the hundred and twenty-seventh; the hundred and thirty-third and the hundred and forty-second. All the rest are to be said at Evensong, and because this leaves three psalms short the longest of them, namely, the hundred and thirty-eighth, the hundred and forty-third, and the hundred and forty-fourth, are to be divided. The hundred and sixteenth, however, since it is brief, is to be joined to the hundred and fifteenth.

The order of the psalms for Evensong being thus arranged, let the other parts, such as the lessons, responsories, hymns, versicles, and canticles, be used as before directed. At Compline the same psalms are repeated every day, namely, the fourth, the ninetieth and the hundred and thirty-third.

The order of the psalmody for the day office being thus settled, all the rest of the psalms are to be equally portioned to the seven night watches (or Matins). Those that are too long are to be divided into two; and twelve psalms are to be arranged for each night. If this distribution of the psalms displease any one we specially desire him to arrange otherwise, if he think something else better, provided that care be taken that every week the whole Psalter of a hundred and fifty psalms be sung, and that at Matins on Sunday it be begun again. Monks, indeed, show themselves in their service too negligent and indevout who sing less than the Psalter, with the usual canticles, once in the week, when we read that our holy Fathers courageously performed in one day what I would that we who are tepid may do in a whole week.

Chapter XIX

Of the Manner of Singing the Office

We believe that the Divine Presence is everywhere, and that the eyes of the Lord behold both the good and the bad in all places. Especially do we believe without any doubt that this is so when we assist at the Divine Office. Let us therefore always be mindful of what the prophet says, *Serve ye the Lord in fear;*[161] *and again sing ye His praises with understanding;*[162] and, *In the sight of angels I will sing praise to Thee.*[163] Wherefore let us consider how it behoveth us to be in the sight of God and the angels, and so let us take our part in the psalmody that mind and voice accord together.

Chapter XX

On Reverence at Prayer

If, when we wish to obtain some favour from those who have the power to help us, we dare not ask except with humility and reverence, how much more reason is there that we should present our petitions to the Lord God of the universe in all lowliness of heart and purity of devotion. We may know for certain that we shall be heard, not because we use many words, but on account of the purity of our hearts and our tears of sorrow. Our prayer, therefore, should be short and pure, unless by some inspiration of

divine grace it be prolonged. All prayer made by the community
in common, however; should be short; and when the prior (that
is, the superior) has given the sign, let all rise together.

Chapter XXI

The Deans of the Monastery

If the community be large let brethren of good repute and
holy lives be chosen from amongst them and appointed
deans. These shall carefully watch over their deaneries in all
things relating to the commandments of God and the injunctions of the abbot. Deans are to be chosen on whom the abbot
may safely rely to share his burdens, and the choice is not to be
determined by their order (in the community) but by the wor-
thiness of their lives and their proved learning. And if perchance
any one of these deans, being puffed up by pride, be found
blameworthy, and after being thrice corrected will not amend,
then let him be put out of office and another more worthy be
substituted. We direct the same in the case of the Provost.

Chapter XXII

How the Monks are to Sleep

All shall sleep in separate beds and each shall receive, according to the appointment of his abbot, bedclothes, fitted to
the condition of his life. If it be possible let them all sleep in a
common dormitory, but if their great number will not allow this
they may sleep in tens or twenties, with seniors to have charge
of them. Let a candle be constantly burning in the room until
morning, and let the monks sleep clothed and girt with girdles
or cords; but they are not to have knives by their sides in their
beds, lest perchance they be injured whilst sleeping. In this way
the monks shall always be ready to rise quickly when the signal
is given and hasten each one to come before his brother to the
Divine Office, and yet with all gravity and modesty.

The younger brethren are not to have their beds next to each other, but amongst those of the elders. When they rise for the Divine Office let them gently encourage one another, because of the excuses made by those that are drowsy.

Chapter XXIII

Of Excommunication for Offences

If any brother be found stubborn, disobedient, proud, murmuring, or in any way acting contrary to the Holy Rule, or contemning the orders of his seniors, let him, according to the precept of our Lord, be secretly admonished by those seniors, once or twice. If he will not amend let him be publicly reproved before all. But if even then he does not correct his faults, let him, if he understand the nature of the punishment, be subject to excommunication. But if he be obstinate he is to undergo corporal punishment.

Chapter XXIV

What the Manner of Excommunication Should Be

The mode of excommunication or punishment should be proportioned to the fault, and the gravity of the fault shall depend on the judgment of the abbot. If any brother be detected in small faults let him be excluded from eating at table with the rest. The punishment of one thus separated from the common table shall be of this kind: in the oratory he shall not intone either psalm or antiphon; neither shall he read any lesson until he has made satisfaction. He shall take his portion of food alone, after the brethren have had their meal, and in such quantity and at such time as the abbot shall think fit. So that if, for example, the brethren take their meal at the sixth hour let him take his at the ninth; if the brethren take theirs at the ninth, let him have his in the evening, till such time as by due satisfaction he obtain pardon.

Chapter XXV

Of Graver Faults

L et the brother who is guilty of some graver fault be excluded both from the common table and from the oratory. None of the brethren shall talk to him or consort with him. Let him be alone at the work which is set him; let him remain in penance and sorrow, and keep before his mind that terrible sentence of the apostle where he says, *Such a one is delivered over to Satan for the destruction of the flesh, that his spirit may be saved in the day of our Lord.*[164] Let him take his food alone, in such quantity and at such time as the abbot shall think fit. Let no one bless him as he passes by, nor ask a blessing on the food that is given him.

Chapter XXVI

Of Such as Keep Company with the Excommunicated Without the Abbot's Order

I f any brother shall presume, without the abbot's order, to have intercourse in any way with an excommunicated brother, to talk with him or send him any message, let him suffer the same penalty of excommunication.

Chapter XXVII

What Care the Abbot Should Have of the Excommunicated

L et the abbot take every possible care of the offending brethren, for *They that are well need not the physician, but they that are sick.*[165] Like a wise physician, therefore, he ought to make use of every remedy; he should send some of the older and wiser brethren as comforters, to console, as it were, in secret their wayward brother, and win him to make humble satisfaction. And let them comfort him that he be not overwhelmed by too great sorrow, but as as the apostle saith, *Let charity be confirmed in him and let all pray for him.*[166]

The abbot ought to take the greatest care and to use all prudence and industry to lose none of the sheep entrusted to him. Let him know that he hath undertaken the care of souls that are sick, and not act the tyrant over such as are well. Let him fear the reproach of the prophet in which God speaks thus, *What ye saw to be fat that ye took to yourselves, and what was diseased that ye threw away.*[167] Let him copy the loving example of the Good Shepherd, who, leaving ninety-nine sheep in the mountains, went to seek the one that had gone astray, and on whose infirmity He took such compassion that He deigned to lay it on His shoulders and carry it back to the flock.[168]

Chapter XXVIII

Of Those Who, Being Often Corrected, Do Not Amend

If any brother does not amend after being often corrected for any fault, and even excommunicated, let a sharper punishment be administered to him, that is, let him be corrected by stripes. And if even after this he shall not correct himself, or being puffed up by pride (which God forbid) shall attempt to defend his doings, then let the abbot act like a wise physician. If after applying the fomentations and ointments of exhortation, the medicine of the Holy Scriptures and the final cautery of excommunication and scourging, he find that his labours have had no effect, then let him try what is more than all this, his own prayer and those of the brethren for him, that the Lord, who can do all things, may work the cure of the sick brother. If he be not healed by this means then let the abbot use the severing knife, according to that saying of the apostle, *Put away the evil one from among you;*[169] and again, *If the faithless one depart, let him depart,*[170] lest one diseased sheep should infect the whole flock.

Chapter XXIX

Whether Brethren Who Leave Their Monastery Must Be Received Back

If the brother, who through his own bad conduct leaves or is expelled from the monastery, shall desire to return, he must first promise full amendment of the fault for which he left it. He may then be received back to the lowest place, that by this his humility may be tried. If he shall again leave he may be received back till the third time, but he shall know that after this all possibility of returning will be denied to him.

Chapter XXX

How Young Children are to be Corrected

Every age and state of intelligence ought to be governed in the way suitable to it. Thus the faults of those who are children or youths, or who cannot understand the seriousness of the penalty of excommunication, shall be punished by rigorous fasting or corrected by sharp stripes.

Chapter XXXI

What Manner of Man the Cellarer of the Monastery Ought to be

Let one of the community be chosen as cellarer of the monastery, who is wise, mature in character, temperate, not a great eater, nor arrogant nor quarrelsome, nor insolent, and not a dawdler, nor wasteful, but one who fears God and is as a Father to the community. Let him have the charge of everything; do nothing without the abbot's order; see to what is commanded, and not make the brethren sad. If any of them shall perchance ask something unreasonable he must not vex him by contemptuously rejecting his request, but humbly and reasonably refuse what he wrongly asks.

Let him look after his own soul, mindful of the Apostolic principle, that *they that ministered well, shall purchase to themselves a good degree.*[171] Let him take every care of the sick, of children, of guests, and of the poor, knowing that without doubt he shall have to render an account of all these on the judgment day.

Let him look upon all the vessels and goods of the monastery as if they were the consecrated chalices of the altar. He must not think anything can be neglected; he must not be covetous, nor a prodigal wasting the goods of the monastery; but let him do everything with forethought and according to the direction of his abbot.

Above all things let him have humility and give a gentle answer to those to whom he can give nothing else, for it is written, *A good word is above the best gift.*[172] Let him take charge of all the abbot shall commit to him, but let him not meddle with anything which is forbidden him. Let him provide the brethren with their appointed allowance of food without impatience or delay, so that they be not driven to offend, being mindful of the divine word which declares the punishment he deserves *Who shall scandalize one of these little ones. It were better for him that a millstone should be hanged about his neck, and that he should be drowned in the depth of the sea.*[173] If the community be large let him be given helpers, by whose aid he may without worry perform the office committed to him. What is given let it be given, and what is asked for let it be asked at suitable times, so that no one be troubled or distressed in the House of God.

Chapter XXXII

Concerning the Iron Tools or other Goods of the Monastery

Let the abbot appoint brethren, of whose life and moral conduct he is sure, to keep the iron tools, the clothes, or other property of the monastery. To these he shall allot the various things to be kept and collected, as he shall deem expedient. The abbot shall hold a list of these things that, as the brethren succeeded each other in their appointed work, he may know what he gives and what he receives back. If any one shall treat the property of the monastery in a slovenly or careless way let him be corrected; if he does not amend let him be subjected to regular discipline.

Chapter XXXIII

Ought Monks to Have Anything of Their Own?

Above all others, let this vice be extirpated in the monastery. No one, without the leave of the abbot, shall presume to give, or receive, or keep as his own, anything whatsoever: neither book, nor tablets, nor pen: nothing at all. For monks are men who can claim no dominion even over their own bodies or wills. All that is necessary, however, they may hope from the Father of the monastery; but they shall keep nothing which the abbot has not given or allowed. All things are to be common to all, as it is written, *Neither did any one say or think that aught was his own.*[174] Hence if any one shall be found given to this most wicked vice let him be admonished once or twice, and if he do not amend let him be subjected to correction.

Chapter XXXIV

Whether All Ought to Receive Necessary Things Uniformly

It is written, *Distribution was made to every one, according as he had need.*[175] By this we do not mean that there is to be a personal preference (which God forbid), but a consideration for infirmities. In this wise let him who needs less thank God and be not distressed, and let him who requires more be humiliated because of his infirmity, and not puffed up by the mercy that is shown him: so all the members shall be in peace. Above all things let not the pest of murmuring, for whatever cause, by any word or sign, be manifested. If any one shall be found faulty in this let him be subjected to the most severe punishment.

Chapter XXXV

Of the Weekly Servers in the Kitchen

The brethren are so to serve each other that no one be excused from the work of the kitchen unless on the score of health, or because he is occupied in some matter of great utility, for thence great reward is obtained and charity is exercised. Let the weaker brethren, however, have help that they may not do their work in sadness; and let all generally be helped according to the circumstances of the community or the position of the place (*i.e.* kitchen). If the community be large the cellarer may be eased from the service of the kitchen, and any others who (as we have said) are engaged in matters of greater utility. Let the rest serve one another in charity. On Saturday, he who ends his weekly service must clean up everything. He must wash the towels with which the brethren wipe their hands and feet; and he who finishes his service, and he who enters on it, are to wash the feet of all. He shall give back to the cellarer all the vessels used in his ministry, cleaned and unbroken, and the cellarer shall hand them to the one entering on his office, that he may know what he gives and what he receives.

An hour before the meal these weekly servers may receive a draught of water and a piece of bread over and above the appointed allowance, so that they may serve the brethren at meal time without murmuring or too great fatigue. On solemn days, however, let them wait till after Mass. Immediately after Lauds on Sunday both the incoming and outgoing servers for the week shall cast themselves on their knees in the presence of all and ask their prayers. Let him who finishes his week say this verse, *Blessed art Thou, O Lord God, who didst help me and consoled me;*[176] and when this has been said three times let him receive a blessing. He who enters on his office shall then follow, and say, *O God, incline unto mine aid; O Lord, make haste to help me;*[177] and this also shall be repeated thrice by all, and having received his blessing let him enter on his service.

Chapter XXXVI

Of the Sick Brethren

Before all things and above all things special care must be taken of the sick, so that in very deed they be looked after as if it were Christ Himself who was served. He Himself has said, *I was sick, and ye visited Me; and what ye did to one of these, My least brethren, ye did to Me.*[178]

But let the sick themselves bear in mind that they are served for the honour of God, and should not grieve their brethren who serve them by their superfluous demands. These, nevertheless, must be borne with patience, since from such a more abundant reward is obtained. Let the abbot, therefore, take the greatest care that the sick suffer no neglect.

For them let a separate cell be set apart with an attendant who is God-fearing, diligent and painstaking. Let baths be granted to the sick as often as it shall be expedient, but to those in health, and especially to the young, they shall be seldom permitted. Also for the recovery of their strength the use of meat may be allowed to the sick and those of very weak health. As soon, however, as they shall mend they must all in the accustomed manner abstain from flesh meat. Let the abbot take special care that the sick be not neglected by the cellarer or the attendants, because he is responsible for what is done amiss by his disciples.

Chapter XXXVII

Concerning Old Men and Children

Although human nature itself inclines us to show pity and consideration to age, to the old, that is, and to children, still it is proper that the authority of the Rule should provide for them. Let their weakness be always taken into account, and let the full rigour of the Rule as regards food be in no wise maintained in their regard. There is to be a kind consideration for them, and permission is to be given them to anticipate the regular hours.

Chapter XXXVIII

The Weekly Reader

There ought always to be reading whilst the brethren eat at table. Yet no one shall presume to read there from any book taken up at haphazard; but whoever is appointed to read for the whole week is to enter on his office on the Sunday. Let the brother when beginning his service after Mass and Communion ask all to pray for him, that God may preserve him from the spirit of pride. And let the following verse be thrice repeated by all in the oratory, he, the reader, first beginning: *O Lord, Thou wilt open my lips, and my mouth shall declare Thy praise,*[179] then, having received a blessing, let the reader enter upon his office. The greatest silence shall be kept, so that no whispering, nor noise, save the voice of the reader alone, be heard there.

Whatever is required for eating and drinking the brethren shall minister to each other so that no one need ask for anything. Yet should anything be wanted it ought to be demanded by sign rather than by word. Let no one ask any question there about what is being read or about anything else, lest occasion be given to the evil one; unless, perhaps, the prior shall wish to say something briefly for the purpose of edification. The brother who is reader for the week may take a mess of potage before beginning to read, on account of Holy Communion, and lest perchance it may be too long for him to fast. He shall eat afterwards with the weekly servers and kitchen helpers. The brethren, however, are not all to read or sing in course, but only such as may edify the hearers.

Chapter XXXIX

Of the Amount of Food

We believe that it is enough to satisfy just requirement if in the daily meals, at both the sixth and ninth hours, there be at all seasons of the year two cooked dishes, so that he who cannot eat of the one may make his meal of the other. Therefore

two dishes of cooked food must suffice for all the brethren, and
if there be any fruit or young vegetables these may be added to
the meal as a third dish. Let a pound weight of bread suffice for
each day, whether there be one meal or two, that is, for both
dinner and supper. If there is to be supper a third of the pound
is to be kept back by the cellarer and given to the brethren at
that meal.

If, however, the community has been occupied in any great
labour it shall be at the will, and in the power of the abbot, if he
think fit, to increase the allowance, so long as every care be
taken to guard against excess, and that no monk be incapacitat-
ed by surfeiting. For nothing is more contrary to the Christian
spirit than gluttony, as our Lord declares, *Take heed to yourselves lest perhaps your hearts be overcharged with surfeiting.*[180] And the same quantity shall not be given to young children, but a lesser amount than to those older; frugality being
maintained in everything. All, save the very weak and sick, are
to abstain wholly from eating the flesh of quadrupeds.

Chapter XL

Of the Measure of Drink

E*very one hath his proper gift from God, one thus, another
thus.*[181] For this reason the amount of other people's food
cannot be determined without some misgiving. Still, having
regard to the weak state of the sick, we think that a pint of wine
a day is sufficient for any one. But let those to whom God gives
the gift of abstinence know that they shall receive their proper
reward. If either local circumstances, the amount of labour, or
the heat of summer require more, it can be allowed at the will
of the prior, care being taken in all things that gluttony and
drunkenness creep not in.

Although we read that "wine is not the drink of monks at all,"
yet, since in our days they cannot be persuaded of this, let us at
least agree not to drink to satiety, but sparingly, *Because wine
maketh even the wise to fall away.*[182]

Chapter XLI

The Hours at Which the Brethren are to Take Their Meals[183]

From the holy feast of Easter until Whitsuntide the brethren shall have their first meal at the sixth hour and their supper at night. But from Whitsuntide, throughout the summer, if the monks have not to work in the fields, nor are oppressed by any great heat, let them fast on Wednesdays and Fridays till None; on the other days they may dine at the sixth hour. Dinner at the sixth hour shall be the rule at the discretion of the abbot, if they have work in the fields, or the heat of the summer be great. Let the abbot so temper and arrange everything that souls may be saved, and that what the brethren do may be done without just complaint.

From September the thirteenth till the beginning of Lent the brethren shall always take their meal at the ninth hour. During Lent, however, until Easter their meal shall be at eventide; but this evening meal shall be so arranged that whilst eating they shall not need lamps, and all things be finished in daylight. Indeed, at all times of the year let the hour of meals, whether of dinner or supper, be so arranged that all things be done by daylight.

Chapter XLII

That No One Shall Speak After Compline

Monks should practise silence at all times, but especially during the night hours. On all days, therefore, whether it be a fast day or otherwise (this shall be the practise). If it be not a fast day, as soon as they shall have risen from supper let all sit together whilst one of them read the *Collations,* or *Lives of the Fathers,* or some other book to edify the hearers. He shall not, however, read the *Heptateuch,* or *Books of Kings,* for at that hour it will not profit weak understandings to listen to this part of Scripture; at other times, however, they may be read. If it be a fast day let the brethren, when Evensong is over, and after a brief interval, come to the reading of the *Collations,* as we have said. Four or five pages are to be read, or as many as time will allow, that during the reading all may come together, even such as have had some work given them to do. When all, therefore, are gathered together let them say Compline, and on coming out from Compline no one shall be permitted to speak at all. If any one shall be found breaking this rule of silence he shall be punished severely, unless the needs of a guest require it, or the abbot shall order something of some one. But even this shall be done with the greatest gravity and moderation.

Chapter XLIII

Of Those Who Come Late to the
Divine Office or to the Table

As soon as the signal for the Divine Office shall be heard each one must lay aside whatever work he may be engaged upon and hasten to it, with all speed, but still with gravity, so as not to cause any light behaviour. Nothing, therefore, shall be put before the Divine Office. If any one shall come to Matins after the *Gloria* of the ninety-fourth Psalm, which on this account we wish to be said slowly and leisurely, he shall not take his place in the choir, but go last of all, or to some place apart which the abbot may appoint for those that so fail in his sight, and of all the brethren, until the Divine Office be ended and he shall have done penance and made public satisfaction.

We have judged it fitting that these should stand last, or in some place apart, in order that, being seen by all, for very shame they may amend. For if they remain outside the oratory some one will, perhaps, return to sleep, or at least sit outside by himself, or setting himself to idle talk give an occasion to the evil one. Let such a one, therefore, come inside, so that he may not lose all, but make amends during the rest of the Office. At the day Hours one who does not come to the "Work of God" till after the verse *(Deus in adjutorium),* and the

Gloria of the first Psalm said said after the verse, shall stand last, according to the rule laid down above. He is not to presume to join the choir of singers until he has made satisfaction, unless, indeed, the abbot, by his permission, allow him to do so; but even then on the condition that he shall afterwards satisfy for his omission.

He who does not come to table before the verse, so that all may say it, and praying together sit down to table at the same time, must be corrected once or twice if this be through his own fault or bad habit. If he do not after this amend he is not to be allowed to share in the common table, but he is to be separated from the company of all the rest and eat alone. Until he makes satisfaction and mend his ways let his portion of wine be taken away from him. He is to undergo the same punishment who is not present at the verse which is said after meals. Let no one presume to take food or drink before or after the regular time; but if something is offered to any one by the prior, and he refuse it, and afterwards wishes to have what he had rejected, or some other thing, let him get neither this nor anything else till he makes proper satisfaction.

Chapter XLIV

How Those Who are Excommunicated Are to Make Satisfaction

He who has been excluded from the oratory and the table for grievous offences is to prostrate himself before the door of the oratory, in silence, at the time when the Divine Office is being celebrated; with his face to the ground let him lie at the feet of all who leave the place. This he shall continue to do until the abbot shall judge that he has made satisfaction. Then, when the abbot ordains, let him cast himself first at the feet of the abbot and then at those of the brethren, that they may pray for him.

Afterwards, if the abbot shall so direct, let him be received into the choir and into the place he shall appoint him. Even so he may not presume to intone a psalm or to read a lesson, or to do anything else in the oratory, unless the abbot again orders it. Moreover, after each Hour, when the Divine Office is ended, let him cast himself on the ground in his place, and in this way make satisfaction until such time as the abbot tells him to cease. Those who are excluded from the table only shall make satisfaction in the oratory, as long as the abbot shall direct, and shall continue to do this till he blesses them and declares it to be sufficient.

Chapter XLV

Of Those Who Blunder in the Oratory

If any one, whilst reciting a psalm, responsory, antiphon or lesson, make any mistake, and do not at once make humble satisfaction for it before all, let him be subjected to greater punishment, as being one who is unwilling to correct by humility what he has done amiss through negligence. For such a fault let children be whipped.

Chapter XLVI

Of Such as Offend in Other Ways

If any one whilst engaged in any work, either in the kitchen, in the cellar, in serving others, in the bakehouse, in the garden, or in any other occupation or place, shall do anything amiss, break or lose anything, or offend in any way whatsoever, and do not come at once to the abbot and community of his own accord to confess his offence and make satisfaction, if afterwards it shall become known by another he shall be more severely punished. If, however, it be a secret sin let him manifest it only to the abbot, or to his spiritual seniors, who know how to heal their own wounds and not to disclose and make public those of others.

Chapter XLVII

On Letting the Hour of Divine Office be Known

Let the duty of giving warning of the time of the Divine Office, both night and day, be that of the abbot. Either he himself shall give the signal or he shall assign this task to some careful brother, so that all things be done at their fixed time. After the abbot those appointed are to intone the psalms and antiphons in turns. No one, however, shall presume either to sing or read except such as can do so to the edification of the hearers. Let him to whom the abbot shall enjoin this duty do it with humility, gravity and fear.

Chapter XLVIII

Of Daily Manual Labour

Idleness is an enemy of the soul. Because this is so the brethren ought to be occupied at specified times in manual labour, and at other fixed hours in holy reading. We therefore think that both these may be arranged for as follows: from Easter to the first of October, on coming out from Prime, let the brethren labour till about the fourth hour.[184] From the fourth till close upon the sixth hour[185] let them employ themselves in reading. On rising from table after the sixth hour let them rest on their beds in strict silence; but if any one shall wish to read, let him do so in such a way as not to disturb any one else.

Let None be said somewhat before the time, about the middle of the eighth hour,[186] and after this all shall work at what they have to do till evening. If, however, the nature of the place or poverty require them to labour at gathering in the harvest, let them not grieve at that, for then are they truly monks when they live by the labour of their hands, as our Fathers and Apostles did. Let everything, however, be done with moderation for the sake of the faint-hearted.

From the first of October till the beginning of Lent let the brethren be occupied in reading till the end of the second hour.[187] At the time Tierce shall be said, after which they shall labour at the work enjoined them till None.[188] At the first signal for the Hour of None all shall cease to work, so as to be ready when the second signal is given. After their meal they shall be employed in reading or on the psalms.

On the days of Lent, from the morning till the end of the third[189] hour, the brethren are to have time for reading, after which let them work at what is set them to do till the close of the tenth hour.[190] During these Lenten days let each one have some book from the library which he shall read through carefully. These books are to be given out at the beginning of Lent.

It is of much import that one or two seniors be appointed to go about the monastery at such times as the brethren are free to read, in order to see that no one is slothful, given to idleness or foolish talking instead of reading, and so not only makes no profit himself but also distracts others. If any such be found (which God forbid) let him be corrected once or twice, and if he amend not let him be subjected to regular discipline of such a character that the rest may take warning. Moreover one brother shall not associate with another at unsuitable hours.

On Sunday also, all, save those who are assigned to various offices, shall have time for reading. If, however, any one be so negligent and slothful as to be unwilling or unable to read or meditate, he must have some work given him, so as not to be idle. For weak brethren, or those of delicate constitutions, some work or craft shall be found to keep them from idleness, and yet not such as to crush them by the heavy labour or to drive them away. The weakness of such brethren must be taken into consideration by the abbot.

Chapter XLIX

The Observance of Lent

The mode of a monk's life ought at all times to favour that of Lenten observance. Since few, however, are capable of this we exhort every one in these days of Lent to guard their lives in all purity, and during this holy season to wash away every negligence of other times. This we shall worthily accomplish if we restrain ourselves from every vice, and give ourselves to tearful prayer, to reading, to heartfelt sorrow and to abstinence. In these days of Lent, therefore, let us of our own accord add something to our usual yoke of service, such as private prayer, abstinence from food and drink. Let every one of his own will with joy of the Holy Ghost offer to God something above the allotted measure, that is, let him deny his body in food, drink, sleep, talking or laughter, and with spiritual joy await the holy feast of Easter. On this condition, however, that each one inform his abbot what it is that he is offering, for what is done without leave of the spiritual Father will be reckoned presumption and vain-glory, and merit no reward. All things, therefore, must be done with the approval of the abbot.

Chapter L

Of the Brethren Who Work at a Distance From the Oratory or Are on a Journey

Those brethren who work at a distance and cannot come to the oratory at the appointed hours, and the abbot judges that this is so, shall say the Divine Office where they are working, kneeling in the fear of God. In the same way, those who are sent on a journey shall not omit the customary hours, but keep them as best they may, and fail not to accomplish this duty of their service.

Chapter LI

Of Brethren Who Go Only a Short Distance

The brother who is sent on an errand and expects to return to his monastery the same day shall not presume to eat outside his house, even though he be asked to do so by any one, unless he be so ordered by his abbot. If he do otherwise let him be excommunicated.

Chapter LII

Concerning the Oratory of the Monastery

Let the Oratory be what its name signifies, and let nothing else be done or discussed there. When the "Work of God" is ended let all depart in strict silence, in the reverence of God, so that the brother who may wish to pray privately may not be hindered by the misconduct of another. If any brother wish to pray privately let him go into the Oratory, without ostentation, and say his prayers, not with a loud voice, but with tears and an earnest heart. Therefore, as has been said, no one is allowed to remain in the Oratory after the Divine Office is ended, unless for the purpose of prayer, lest some other brother be hindered by him.

Chapter LIII

On the Reception of Guests

Let all guests who come be received as Christ would be, because He will say, *I was a stranger, and ye took Me in.*[191] And let due honour be shown to all, especially to those who are of the household of the Faith, and to pilgrims. As soon, therefore, as a guest is announced let him be met by the prior or the brethren, with all the marks of charity. And let them first pray together, that so they may associate in peace. The kiss of peace, however, is not to be given till after prayer, on account of the deceptions practised by the devil. And in the salutation itself let true humility be shown to all guests coming and going. By bowed head, or body prostrate on the ground, all shall adore Christ in them, Who, indeed, is received in their persons.

Let guests, after their reception, be conducted to prayer, and then the prior, or any one he may order, shall sit with them. Let the Divine Law be read in the presence of the guest for his edification, and after this let all courtesy be shown to him. For the guest's sake the prior may break his fast, unless it be a strict day when the fast may not be broken. The brethren, however, shall keep the accustomed fasts. Let the abbot pour water on the hands of the guests, and let him and all the community wash their feet. After this let them say the verse, *We have received Thy mercy, O God, in the midst of Thy temple.*[192] Let special care be taken of the poor and pilgrims, because in them Christ is more truly received, for the very awe of the rich secures respect for them.

Let the kitchen of the abbot and the guests be apart, so that strangers, who are never absent from a monastery, coming in at irregular hours, may not disturb the community. Let two of the brethren, who can perform their duties well, take charge of this kitchen for a year at a time. When they need it they shall be given assistance, so that they may serve without murmuring. In like manner, when they have lighter work, let them labour where they are told. And, indeed, not only in their regard, but also in respect to all the other officers of the monastery let this consideration be always shown; when they need help let them have it, and when, on the other hand, they are free they shall do what they are ordered. Also, let the charge of the guest-place be assigned to a brother whose soul the fear of God possesses. A sufficient number of beds are to be prepared there, and let the House of God be wisely ruled by wise men.

No one, unless ordered, may associate with or speak to the guests. If any one shall meet or see them, after such humble salutation as we have above enjoined, having asked their blessing, let him pass on, saying he is not permitted to talk with any guest.

Chapter LIV

Whether a Monk May Receive Letters or Presents

It is by no means lawful, without the abbot's permission, for any monk to receive or give letters, presents, and gifts of any kind to any one, whether parent or other, and not even to one of the brethren. If anything is sent to a monk from his parents he shall not venture to receive it unless the abbot be first told. If he order it to be accepted he may appoint the person to whom it shall be given. And let not the brother, to whom perchance it was sent, be grieved, lest an opening be given to the devil. He who shall dare to do otherwise shall be subjected to regular discipline.

Chapter LV

Of the Clothes and Shoes of the Brethren

Let clothing suitable to the locality and the temperature be given to the brethren, for in cold regions more is needed, and less in warm. The determination of all these things is in the hands of the abbot. We believe, however, that in ordinary places it will be enough for each monk to have a cowl and tunic; in winter the cowl being of thicker stuff, in summer of finer or old cloth. He should have also a scapular for working purposes, and shoes and stockings for the feet.

Monks must not grumble at the colour or coarseness of these things; they shall be such as can be procured in the district where they live, or such as can be bought at the cheapest price.

Let the abbot see to their dimensions, that they be not too short, but of the proper length for those who use them. When receiving new clothes the monks shall always give back the old ones at the same time, to be put away in the clothes-room for the poor. For it is sufficient that a monk have two tunics and two cowls, as well for night wear as for the convenience of washing. Anything beyond this is superfluous, and must be cut off. Their shoes also, and whatever is worn out, they shall return on getting new things. Those who are sent on a journey shall get hosen from the wardrobe, which, on their return, when washed, they shall restore. Let their cowls and tunics on such occasions be somewhat better than those in ordinary use. These they shall receive from the wardrobe when starting and restore on their return.

A mattress, blanket, coverlet and pillow are to suffice for bedding. The beds shall be frequently searched by the abbot to guard against the vice of hoarding. And if any one be found in possession of something not allowed by the abbot let him be subjected to the severest punishment. And to uproot this vice of appropriation let all that is necessary be furnished by the abbot, that is, cowl, tunic, shoes, stockings, girdle, knife, pen, needle, handkerchief and tablets. By this every pretext of necessity will be taken away. The abbot, however, should always bear in mind that sentence in the Acts of the Apostles, *And distribution was made to every one according as he had need.*[193] He should, therefore, consider the infirmities of such as need something, and not regard the ill-will of the envious. In all his decisions let him ponder upon the retribution of God.

Chapter LVI

The Abbot's Table

The abbot shall always take his meals with the guests and strangers. But when there are few guests, he may invite any of the brethren he may choose. Let him see, however, that one or two of the seniors be always left with the community, for the sake of discipline.

Chapter LVII

Of the Artificers of the Monastery

Let such craftsmen as be in the monastery ply their trade in all lowliness of mind, if the abbot allow it. But if any be puffed up by his skill in his craft, and think the monastery indebted to him for it, such a one shall be shifted from his handicraft, and not attempt it again till such time as, having learnt a low opinion of himself, the abbot shall bid him resume. If aught of the fruit of their labours be sold let them that have the handling of the affair see to it that they do not dare to practise any fraud therein.

Let them remember Ananias and Saphira,[194] lest they, or any who practise any fraud in regard to the possessions of the monastery, suffer the death of their souls as did they of their bodies. In settling the prices, however, do not let the vice of greed creep in, but let the things be sold somewhat cheaper than they can be by laymen, that in all things God may be glorified.

Chapter LVIII

The Manner of Receiving the Brethren to Religion

Any one on the first coming to the religious life should not find the entrance made easy, but as the apostle saith, *Try the spirits, if they be of God.*[195] If, however, the newcomer continues to knock, and for four or five days shows a patient bearing, both of the harshness shown him and of the difficulty made about admitting him, and persist in his petition he shall then be allowed to enter the guest-place for a few days. After that let him be in the noviciate, where he shall meditate and eat and sleep.

And let a senior, such as has the skill of winning souls, be appointed to watch carefully over him, to discover whether he truly seeks God and is eager for the Divine Office, for obedience and humiliations. Let all the rigour and austerity of our journey to God be put clearly before him. If he promise to continue in a steadfast perseverance, at the end of two months the entire Rule shall be read to him, and let him be told, "See the law under which you wish to fight, if you can observe it enter upon the life; if you cannot you are free to depart."

If he still persevere let him be brought back to the noviciate and again tried in all patience. And after the lapse of six months let the Rule be read to him again, that he may fully know the kind of life he is entering upon. If he yet persevere, after four months the Rule shall be read to him once more. If after due deliberation he shall then promise to keep all the law and to do whatever is commanded of him, let him be received into the community, knowing that he is now under the law of the Rule, so that he can henceforth neither leave the monastery nor withdraw his neck from the yoke of the Rule which after so long a deliberation he was free to have taken or refused.

When he is to be admitted into the community let him in the oratory, and in the presence of all, promise before God and His saints stability, amendment of manners and obedience, in order that if at any time he shall act otherwise he may know that he shall be condemned by Him Whom he mocketh. He shall draw up the form of his promise in the name of the saints, whose relics are reposing there, and of the abbot there present. Let him write out this form himself, or at least, if he is uneducated another at his request must write it for him, and to this the novice himself shall set his mark and with his own hand lay it upon the altar.

After he has placed it there let the novice immediately begin the verse, *Uphold me, O Lord, according to Thy word, and I shall live, and let me not be confounded in my expectation.*[196] This verse the community shall repeat three times, adding at the end, *Glory be to the Father,* etc. Then the brother novice shall cast himself at the feet of all, asking their prayers, and from that time he shall be counted as one of the community. If he has any property he must first either give it to the poor, or by formal gift make it over to the monastery without any reservation for himself, since he must know that he has henceforth no power even over his own body. Let him, therefore, forthwith be divested in the oratory of his own garments and be clothed in those of the monastery. The clothes he has taken off, however, are to be kept in the wardrobe, so that if (which God forbid) he should, by the persuasion of the devil, resolve to leave the monastery he may be stripped of his monastic dress and expelled. The form of profession which the abbot took from him at the altar he shall not receive back, but it shall be kept in the monastery.

Chapter LIX

Of the Sons of Nobles or of the Poor Who are Offered to God

If any nobleman shall offer his son to God in the monastery, let the parents, if the child himself be under age, make the petition for him, and together with the oblation wrap the formal promise and the hand of the boy in the altar cloth and thus dedicate him to God. With regard to any property let the parents promise in the document under oath that they will never either give or furnish him with the means of obtaining anything whatever, either themselves or by any other person or by any means. Or, if they will not do this, and desire to give some alms to the monastery, as a free gift, let them hand over to the place what they wish, reserving, if they please, the income for themselves. Let all these matters be so managed that the child have no expectations by which he may be deceived and perish (which God forbid), as by experience we have learnt is sometimes the case. In the same way let those who are poorer act. But such as have nothing whatever shall simply make the promise and offer their son before witnesses with the oblation.

Chapter LX

Of Priests Who Wish to Dwell in the Monastery

If any one in the ranks of the priesthood shall ask to be received into a monastery let him not obtain permission too quickly. If, however, he persist in his request he shall understand that he will have to keep the Rule in all rigour, and that no mitigation will be allowed to him, according to what is written, *Friend, for what art thou come?* Nevertheless let him be allowed to stand next after the abbot, to give the blessing or to say Mass, provided the abbot order him. If not, he may not presume to do aught, knowing that he is subject to the discipline of regular life, and is specially obliged to set an example of humility to all. If perchance his position in the monastery shall have been given him because of his Orders, or for any other reason, he should remember that his proper place is what he has by the time of his entry to the monastery, not that which is given him out of respect for the priesthood. But if any clerics manifest the same desire to be admitted into the monastery let them be put into a middle rank, but only if they give promise of observance of the Rule and of their stability therein.

Chapter LXI

Of Monks Who are Strangers,
How They Are to Be Received

If any stranger monk, coming from a distant place, desire to dwell in the monastery as a guest and, content with the customs he there finds, does not trouble the house by superfluous wants, but is simply content with what he finds, let him be received for as long a time as he desires to remain. And if he reasonably and with loving humility blames something, or points out anything amiss, let the abbot prudently consider it, lest perchance the Lord shall have sent him there for that purpose. If, also, after a time he shall wish to make his stay permanent, such a desire should not be refused, particularly since during the time he has lived as a guest his manner of life could be known.

If in that period he shall have been found troublesome or vicious, not only should he not be incorporated with the community, but he should even be told frankly to leave, lest others be corrupted by his ill doing. But if he does not deserve to be sent away, not only if he shall ask, shall he be received into the ranks of the community, but he should even be induced to stay, that others may be taught by his example, because in every place we serve a common Lord, and fight under the same King.

And if the abbot shall find such a monk deserving he may even put him into a somewhat higher rank. And the abbot may raise above the rank of his entry into religion, not only any monk, but also any of the foresaid priests or clerics, if he shall consider that their lives deserve it. Let the abbot, however, beware never to receive permanently any monk of a known monastery without the consent of his own abbot, or without letters of commendation from him, for it is written, *What thou wilt not have done to thyself, do not to another.*[197]

Chapter LXII

The Priests of the Monastery

If any abbot desire to have a priest or deacon ordained let him choose from his monks one who is worthy to fill the office of priesthood. Let the monk, however, who is ordained beware of haughtiness and pride, and let him not presume to do anything except what is ordered by the abbot, remembering that he is now much more subject to regular discipline. Let him not make his priesthood an excuse for forgetting obedience and the rigour of the Rule, rather he should strive on account of it to draw more and more towards God.

He shall, moreover, always keep the place he had when he came to the monastery, except in his service at the altar, or if on account of the holiness of his life, by the wish of the community and the will of the abbot, he be moved up to a higher place. Even then let him understand that he must keep the rules prescribed for him by the deans or provosts, and if he presume to act otherwise he shall be judged not as a priest but as a rebel. If after frequent warnings he shall not amend his ways, even the bishop shall be brought in to witness to the fact. And if after this he does not amend, and his faults become notorious, let him be expelled from the monastery, if his contempt be such that he will not submit and obey the Rule.

Chapter LXIII

The Order of the Community

The brethren shall take their places according to the date of their conversion, the merit of their lives, or the appointment of their abbot. And the abbot must not disturb the flock committed to him, nor, as it were, by any arbitrary use of his power, ordain anything unjustly. But let him always remember that he will have to render an account to God of all his judgments and of all his works.

Wherefore in the order he shall appoint, or in that which they hold amongst themselves, let the brethren receive the Pax, approach Communion, intone a psalm and stand in choir. In all places, without exception, order shall not be decided by age, for this shall not be a prejudice to any one, since Samuel and Daniel, though children, were judges of the priests.[198] With the exception therefore of those who, as we have said, for some weighty reason, the abbot shall advance, or for certain causes shall put in a lower place, let all the rest remain in the order of their conversion. For example, one who shall come to the monastery at the second hour of the day shall know that he is junior to him who has come at the first hour, no matter what his age or dignity may be. In regard to children, let them be kept by all under discipline in every way.

Let the juniors, therefore, honour their seniors, and the seniors love the juniors. In addressing each other in person no one shall call another by his mere name, but let the senior call the junior, *Brother,* and the junior call the senior, *Father.* But, because the abbot is held to take the place of Christ, he shall be called *Sir* and *Abbot,* not out of consideration for himself, but for the honour and love of Christ. He, however, should remember and so conduct himself as to be worthy of such an honour.

Wherever the brethren meet each other the junior shall ask a blessing from the senior. When a senior passes by let the junior rise and make place for him to sit down; neither shall the junior presume to sit unless the senior bid him so to do, in order to fulfil what is written, *In honour preventing one another.*[199]

Little children or youths shall keep their respective places in the oratory and at table, under discipline. Outside watch shall be kept over them, everywhere indeed, till they come to an age of understanding.

Chapter LXIV

The Election of the Abbot

In the election of an abbot let the following points be always borne in mind: that he be made abbot whom the whole community, in the fear of God, make choice of, or a part of it, however small, acting with greater wisdom. Let him who is created abbot be chosen because of his virtuous life and his wisdom, even if he be the last in the community. And although the whole community (which God forbid) shall unanimously choose one who supports them in their evil practices, and their vicious lives become known to the bishop (to whose diocese the monastery belongs), or to the abbots or Christians of the neighbourhood, they shall annul the choice of these bad men and appoint a worthy steward of God's House, knowing that for this they shall receive a good reward, provided they do it with pure intention and through zeal of God, just as, on the other hand, they sin if they neglect to do it.

Let him who has been created abbot ever reflect upon the weighty burden he has taken up and remember unto Whom he shall give an account of his stewardship. Let him know also that it is better for him to profit others than to rule over them. He must therefore be learned in the Divine Law that he may know when to *bring forth new things and old.*[200] He must be chaste, sober, merciful, and always exalt mercy above justice, that he may obtain mercy. He shall hate vice and love the brethren. Even in his correction he shall act with prudence and not try too much, lest whilst too violently scouring off the rust the vessel itself be broken. Let him always bear in mind his own frailty, and remember that *the bruised reed must not be broken.*[201]

In saying this we do not propose that he should allow vices to spring up, but, as we have declared before, seek to root them up prudently and with charity, in the way he shall think proper in each case. Let him aim at being loved rather than feared. He must not be worried nor anxious, neither should he be too exacting or obstinate, or jealous, or over-suspicious, for then he will never be at rest. Even in what he orders, whether it relates to God or to worldly matters, let him be prudent and considerate. In all that he enjoins he should be discreet and moderate, meditating on the prudence of holy Jacob, who says, *If I shall cause my flocks to be over-driven, they will all die in one day.*[202] Wherefore adopting these and like principles of discretion, the mother of virtues, let him so temper all things that the strong may have their scope and the weak be not scared. And especially let him keep the present Rule in all things, so that when he shall have well administered it he may hear from our Lord what the good servant heard who gave corn to his fellow-servants in due season: *Amen; I say to you, over all his goods will he place him.*[203]

Chapter LXV

The Provost of the Monastery

It often happens that by the appointment of a provost grave scandals arise in monasteries. Some there are who, puffed up by the evil spirit of pride, and esteeming themselves to be like abbots, take on themselves to act the tyrant, to foster scandals and promote discord in the community. This is specially the case in places where the provost is appointed by the same priests or abbots who appoint the abbot of the monastery. How foolish this custom is may easily be seen. From the very commencement of the appointment a pretext for pride is given to the provost, since his imagination suggests to him that he is now released from the power of his abbot, for (as it seems to say) "You are appointed by those who created the abbot." Hence arise envy, quarrels, detractions, rivalries and disorders. And whilst the abbot and the provost are at variance it must of necessity follow that their souls are endangered by the quarrel, and that those under them, by taking sides, are going to destruction. The guilt of this danger chiefly weighs on those who were the authors of such appointments.

Therefore we foresee that for the preservation of peace and charity it is expedient that the ordering of his monastery depend on the will of the abbot. And, as we have before arranged, if it be possible, let all the work of the monastery be managed by deans, as we have directed, in order that where many are entrusted with the work no one may become proud.

But if the circumstances of the place require a provost, or the community shall with reason and humility ask for one, and the abbot shall think it expedient, with the advice of the brethren who have the fear of God, let him nominate whomsoever he shall himself choose as provost. Let this provost, moreover, reverently do whatever shall be enjoined him by his abbot, never acting against his will or directions, because the higher he is raised above the others the more careful he must be to keep the precepts of the Rule. If this provost shall be found viciously inclined, or carried away by the haughtiness of pride, or a proved despiser of the Holy Rule, let him be warned four times; if he does not amend let him fall under the punishment of regular discipline. If even then he be not corrected he shall be deposed from his position of provost, and another who is worthy shall be put in his place. If after this he shall not be quiet and obedient in the community let him even be put out of the monastery. The abbot nevertheless shall bear in mind that he will have to give an account of all his judgments to God, lest perchance his soul may burn with the flame of envy and jealousy.

Chapter LXVI

The Porter of the Monastery

Let there be stationed at the gate of the monastery some wise old man who knows how to give and receive an answer, and whose age will not allow him to wander from his post. This porter should have his cell near the door, that those who arrive may always find him there to give an answer.

As soon as any one shall knock, or some poor man shall call for help, let him reply, *Thanks be to God,* or invoke a blessing. And let him in the meekness of God's fear hasten to reply with zealous charity. If the porter stands in need of help let him have a junior brother with him. The monastery, however, itself ought, if possible, to be so constructed as to contain within it all necessaries, that is water, mill, garden and [places for] the various crafts which are exercised within a monastery, so that there be no occasion for monks to wander abroad, since this is in no wise expedient for their souls. We wish this Rule to be read frequently in the community so that no brother may plead ignorance as an excuse.

Chapter LXVII

Of Brethren Sent On a Journey

When brethren are about to be sent on a journey let them commend themselves to the prayers of all the brethren and of the abbot, and at the closing prayer of the Divine Office let a commemoration be made of all the absent brethren. When they come back from a journey, on the day of their return, at all the Canonical Hours when the Divine Office is finished, the brethren shall prostrate themselves on the ground and beg the prayers of all for any faults they may have fallen into on the road, by the sight or hearing of evil things, or by idle discourse. And let no one dare to relate to another what he shall have seen or heard outside the monastery, because this is most detrimental. If an one shall presume to do this he must be subjected to the punishment prescribed in the Rule. In like manner shall he be punished who shall presume to break the enclosure of the monastery, or go anywhere, or do anything, however trifling, without the abbot's permission.

Chapter LXVIII

When a Brother is Ordered to Do Impossibilities

If anything hard or impossible be enjoined on a brother let him receive the injunctions of him who orders him in all mildness and obedience. If he shall see that the burden altogether exceedeth the measure of his strength let him patiently and at the proper time state, without show of pride, resistance or contradiction, the reason of this impossibility. If after his suggestion the will of the prior shall still remain unchanged, let the young monk know that it is best for him; and trusting in God's help, through love of Him, let him obey.

Chapter LXIX

That in the Monastery No One
Presume to Defend Another

Special care must be taken that under no pretext one monk presume to defend or uphold another in a monastery, even though they may be very near akin. In no way whatsoever let monks dare to do this, because from it an occasion of the gravest scandal may arise. If any one shall transgress in this way he shall be severely punished.

Chapter LXX

That No One Presume to Strike Another

In the monastery every occasion of presumption should be avoided. We ordain that no one shall be allowed to excommunicate or strike any of his brethren unless the abbot has given him authority to do so. Those who offend in this matter shall be reprehended before all, that the rest may be inspired with fear. But over children, till they are fifteen years old, let all exercise strict discipline and care, yet this also must be done with moderation and discretion. He, however, who shall presume to do so to those above this age, without the abbot's order, or shall be severe to children beyond discretion, shall be subjected to regular discipline, since it is written, *What thou wouldst not have done to thyself, do not thou to another.*[204]

Chapter LXXI

That the Brethren be Obedient to Each Other

The excellent virtue of obedience is to be shown by all, not to the abbot only, but to the brethren who shall also mutually obey each other, knowing that by this path of obedience they shall go to God. The commands of the abbot, or other superiors constituted by him, having the first place (for to these we do not allow any private orders to be preferred) the juniors shall obey their seniors with all charity and diligence. If any one be found contentious let him be punished.

If a brother be rebuked for even the least thing by the abbot, or by any prior (*i.e.* superior), or if he shall perceive that the mind of any superior is, however slightly, moved against him, or in anger with him, let him without delay prostrate himself at his feet, and remain offering satisfaction until the feeling be removed and he receive a blessing. If any one be found too proud to do this let him be expelled from the monastery.

Chapter LXXII

Of the Good Zeal Monks Should Have

As there is an evil and bitter emulation which separates from God and leads to hell, so there is a good spirit of emulation which frees from vices and leads to God and life everlasting. Let monks therefore practise this emulation with most fervent love; that is to say, let them *in honour prevent one another,*[205] let them bear most patiently with each other's infirmities, whether of body or of manner. Let them contend with one another in their obedience. Let no one follow what he thinks most profitable to himself, but rather what is best for another. Let them show brotherly charity with a chaste love. Let them fear God and love their abbot with sincere and humble affection, and set nothing whatever before Christ, Who can bring us unto eternal life.

Chapter LXIII

That All Perfection is Not Contained in This Rule

We have written this Rule, that, by its observance in monasteries, we may show that we have in some measure uprightness of manners or the beginning of religious life. But for such as hasten onward to the perfection of holy life there are the teachings of the Holy Fathers, the observance whereof leads a man to the heights of perfection. For what page or what passage of the divinely inspired books of the Old and the New Testament is not a most perfect rule for man's life? Or what book is there of the Holy Catholic Fathers that doth not proclaim this, that by a direct course we may come to our Creator? Also, what else are the *Collations* of the Fathers, their Institutes, their *Lives,* and the Rule of our Holy Father St. Basil, but examples of the virtues, of the good living and obedience of monks? But to us who are slothful, and lead bad and negligent lives, they are matter for shame and confusion.

Do thou, therefore, whosoever thou art who hasteneth forward to the heavenly country, accomplish first, by the help of Christ, this little Rule written for beginners, and then at length shalt thou come, under God's guidance, to the lofty heights of doctrine and virtue, which we have spoken of above.

Notes

[1] The beginning of this Prologue suggests that St. Benedict had before him in writing the Latin translation of St. Basil's *Admonitio ad filium spiritualem,* which commences with the words "Audi fili admonitionem patris tui, et inclina aurem tuam." The invitation in the Prologue to the Rule is considerably longer than that of St. Basil's tract.

[2] I Rom. xiii. 2.

[3] Ps. xciv. 8.

[4] Apoc. ii. 7.

[5] Ps. xxxiii. 12.

[6] Joan. xii. 35.

[7] Ps. xxxiii. 13

[8] Ps. xxxiii. 14, 15.

[9] Isai. lxv. 24.

[10] Eph. vi. 14, 15.

[11] Ps. xiv. 4.

[12] Ps. xiv. 2, 3.

[13] Ps. cxiii. 1.

[14] 1 Cor. xv. 10.

[15] 2 Cor. x. 47.

[16] Matth. vii. 24 *seq.*

[17] Rom. ii. 4.

[18] Ezech. xviii. 23.

[19] Matth. vii. 13.

[20] 2 Cor. i. 7.

[21] The Rule is written for monks who live together in community life under an abbot. This method of life St. Benedict considers the best to attain the end of all religious life, the realization of the supernatural and the closer union of the soul with God. For this reason he calls those who lead the cenobital or community life the *fortissimum genus.*

[22] Rom. viii. 15.

[23] Ps. xxxix. 11.

[24] Isai. i. 2.

[25] 1 Cor. ix. 27.

[26] Ps. xlix. 16, 17.

[27] Matth. vii. 3.

[28] 1 Cor. xii. 13.

[29] Eph. vi. 9.

[30] 2 Tim. iv. 2.

[31] 1 Reg. ii. 11, 12.

[32] Prov. xxiii. 13.

[33] Prov. xxiii. 14.

[34] Matth. vi. 33.
[35] Ps. xxxiii. 19.
[36] Eccl. xxxii. 24.
[37] Deut. vi. 5.
[38] Luc. x. 27.
[39] Luc. xviii. 20.
[40] Matth. xix. 18.
[41] Exod. xx. 15.
[42] Deut. vi. 21.
[43] Marc. x. 19.
[44] 1 Pet. ii. 17.
[45] Tob. iv. 16.
[46] Luc. ix. 23.
[47] 1 Cor. ix. 27.
[48] 2 Pet. ii. 13.
[49] Joel i. 14.
[50] Tob. iv. 7.
[51] Is. lviii. 7.
[52] Matth. xxv. 36.
[53] Tob. i. 21.
[54] Is. i. 17.
[55] 1 Thes. v. 14.
[56] Jac. i. 27.
[57] Matth. x. 38.
[58] Matth. v. 22.
[59] Eph. iv. 26.
[60] Ps. xiv. 3.
[61] Rom. xii. 18.
[62] 1 Pet. iv. 8.
[63] Matth. v. 33–37.
[64] Ps. xiv. 3.
[65] 1 Thes. v. 15.
[66] 1 Cor. vi. 7.
[67] Luc. vi. 27.
[68] 1 Pet. iii. 9.
[69] Matth. v. 10.
[70] Tob. iv. 14.
[71] 1 Tim. iii. 3.
[72] Eccl. xxxi. 17.
[73] Prov. xx. 13.
[74] Rom. xii. 11.
[75] 1 Cor. x. 10.

[76] Sap. i. 11.
[77] Ps. lxxii. 28.
[78] 1 Cor. iv. 7.
[79] Os. xii. 9.
[80] Job xxxi. 14.
[81] Matth. x. 28.
[82] Phil. i. 23.
[83] Matth. xxiv. 42.
[84] Deut. iv. 9.
[85] Prov. v. 21.
[86] Ps. cxxxvi. 9.
[87] Eccl. viii. 11.
[88] Ps. xxxiii. 13.
[89] Prov. x. 19.
[90] Matth. xii. 36.
[91] Eccl. xxi. 23.
[92] Luc. xi. 28.
[93] Col. iv. 2.
[94] Ps. vi. 7.
[95] Gal. v. 16.
[96] Eccl. xviii. 30.
[97] Matth. xxiii. 30.
[98] Matth. vi. 1.
[99] Eccl. vi. 37.
[100] 1 Tim. v. 22.
[101] Levit. xix. 17.
[102] James iii. 14–16.
[103] 2 Tim. ii. 24.
[104] Ps. cxxx. 1.
[105] Levit. xix. 32.
[106] 1 Tim. v. 1.
[107] Matth. v. 44.
[108] Eph. iv. 26.
[109] Ps. li. 10.
[110] 1 Cor. ii. 9.
[111] Ps. xvii. 45.
[112] Luc. x. 16.
[113] Matth. vii. 14.
[114] Jo. v. 30.
[115] Luc. x. 16.
[116] 2 Cor. ix. 7.
[117] Ps. xxxviii. 2, 3.

[118] Prov. xviii. 21.

[119] Luv. xiv. 11.

[120] Ps. cxxx. 1, 2.

[121] Ps. vii. 10.

[122] Ps. xciii. 11.

[123] Ps. cxxxviii. 3.

[124] Ps. lxxv. 11.

[125] Ps. xvii. 24.

[126] Eccl. xviii. 30.

[127] Matth. vi. 10.

[128] Prov. xvi. 25.

[129] Ps. lii. 2.

[130] Ps. xxxvii. 10.

[131] Eccl. xviii. 30.

[132] Ps. lii. 4.

[133] Ps. xlix. 21.

[134] Jo. vi. 38.

[135] Phil. ii. 8.

[136] Matth. xxiv. 13.

[137] Ps. xxvi. 14.

[138] Ps. xliii. 22.

[139] Rom. viii. 37.

[140] Ps. lxv. 10, 11.

[141] Ps. lxv. 12.

[142] 2 Cor. xi. 26.

[143] Ps. xxxvi. 5.

[144] Ps. cv. 1.

[145] Ps. xxxi. 5.

[146] Ps. lxxii. 22, 23.

[147] Ps. xxi. 7.

[148] Ps. lxxxvii. 16.

[149] Ps. cxviii. 7.

[150] Prov. x. 19.

[151] Ps. cxxxix. 12.

[152] Eccl. xxi. 23.

[153] Eccl. x. 14.

[154] Luc. xviii. 13.

[155] Ps. cxviii. 107.

[156] Ps. lxix. 2.

[157] Ps. l. 17.

[158] The number of twelve psalms is said to have been revealed to the Fathers of the desert when they were uncertain what number to say for the night office. (Cf. Cass. Coll. Lib. ii. c. 5).

[159] Ps. cxviii. 164.

[160] Ps. cxviii. 62.

[161] Ps. ii. 11.

[162] Ps xlvi. 8.

[163] Ps. cxxxvii. 1.

[164] 1. Cor. v. 5.

[165] Matth. ix. 12.

[166] 2 Cor. ii. 8.

[167] Ezech. xxxiv. 3.

[168] Luc. xv. 4.

[169] 1 Cor. v. 13.

[170] 1 Cor. vii. 15.

[171] 1 Tim. iii. 13.

[172] Eccl. xviii. 17.

[173] Matth. xviii. 6.

[174] Acts iv. 32.

[175] Acts iv. 35.

[176] Ps. lxxxv. 18.

[177] Ps. lxix. 2.

[178] Matth. xxv. 36–40.

[179] Ps. l. 17.

[180] Luc. xxi. 34.

[181] 1 Cor. vii. 7.

[182] Eccl. xix. 2.

[183] It may be useful here to say something about the hours named in the Rule. The division of time, according to the Romans, was into twelve hours for the day and twelve for the night. The length of the hour, however, varied according to the seasons of the year, the division of day and night being different: in winter the night hours were longer than the day hours, in summer they were shorter. That is, in

winter, each hour of the night was roughly eighty minutes, and each hour of the day forty minutes. In saying, therefore, that the night office was to begin at the eighth hour, from November to Easter, St. Benedict probably intended to indicate our 3 a.m. (Cap. viii). Lauds was always to begin "about the break of day." In the summer months this would be about 3.30 to 4, and Matins would be during that time, probably about 2.30–3 a.m.

In the same way the midday meal in the summer time was to be at the sixth hour of the day, or midday. From September 13 to the beginning of Lent the dinner was to be at the ninth hour, or from 1.20–2 o'clock, and during Lent the one meal was to be taken in the evening, at such a time as "all be done by daylight." This, allowing for an interval after the meal, and for Compline, would put the single meal at about our 5 o'clock (Cap. xli.).

[184] The fourth hour would have been in summer about 9.20 a.m.

[185] The sixth hour would have been about midday.

[186] None would thus be said about 3.20 p.m.

[187] In the winter months the end of the second hour would correspond to our 9.20 a.m.

[188] *i.e.* 1.20 p.m.

[189] *i.e.* 10 p.m.

[190] *i.e.* 2.40 p.m.

[191] Matth. xxv. 35.

[192] Ps. xlvii. 10.

[193] Acts iv. 35.

[194] Acts v. 1–10.

[195] 1 Jo. iv. 1.

[196] Ps. cxviii. 116.

[197] Matth. vii. 12.

[198] 1 Reg. vii. 15, cf Dan. xiii. 51, *seqq.*

[199] Rom. xii. 10.

[200] Matth. xiii. 52.

[201] Is. xlii. 3.

[202] Gen. xxxiii. 13.

[203] Matth. xxiv. 47.

[204] Tob. iv. 16.

[205] Rom xii. 10.